Narcissism

What You Need to Know about Narcissists and How They Use Manipulation Techniques such as Gaslighting to Control You

Contents

Part 1: Narcissists

The Ultimate Guide to Understanding Narcissism and Ways of Dealing With a Narcissist Who Is Using Manipulation at Work or in an Abusive Relationship

NARCISSISTS

The Ultimate Guide to Understanding
Narcissism and Ways of Dealing With a
Narcissist Who Is Using Manipulation
at Work or in an Abusive Relationship

TYRON BRADEN

Introduction

Narcissism is a hot topic right now. Everyone seems to be talking about it, and there are tons of books being published on the topic. What makes this book different from the other books out there? Many hours of research have gone into this book, and it contains the latest information. More than that, this book is not about teaching you how to diagnose a narcissist clinically, but instead, it is about showing you how you can identify the narcissists in your life.

Narcissists can cause unseen damage. They are masters of disguise. They make us feel that we are safe and loved in the beginning, only to turn on us and cause us pain. Maybe you have someone in your life that you think may be a narcissist. Maybe you are wondering if a specific person in your life displays narcissistic tendencies.

It can be hard to identify a narcissist by their behavior early on in a relationship. They can come across as confident and motivated. They can be extremely successful, which can make it hard to believe that they are narcissists or that they could abuse you.

Growing up with a narcissist in your family can make you feel as if you have nowhere to turn. You may feel that they can convince everyone else that *you* are the problem. They can make you feel that you are completely alone. By identifying the narcissist, you are going to be able to take the control back from them, and that is exactly what you are going to learn how to do in this book.

Narcissists thrive on being in control. They want someone in their life that is going to do exactly what they say right when they say it. How do they find these people? How does a narcissist choose their target? By understanding the answers to these questions, you will be able to protect yourself from narcissists now and in the future.

This book was created with you in mind. So many people want to focus on the narcissist; they seem to be obsessed with what motivates a narcissist and want to know the inner workings of the narcissist's brain. I feel that we should focus on the person that the narcissist targets. Ensuring that you are no longer the victim of a narcissist and helping you to move forward with your life is much more important and much more fascinating than why a narcissist does what they do.

Throughout this book, you will hear stories of Todd and Stacy. Todd is a narcissist; Stacy is his partner. You will see how Stacy was able to identify Todd's behavior and start protecting herself from his abusive tendencies. You will learn how you can do that as well.

Most importantly, you will learn what to do if you are the victim of a narcissist, how you can move forward with your life, and where you can find help.

Chapter One: Understanding Personality

"She has such a great personality." Have you ever heard someone say this? Maybe you have said it yourself. It is something that most people say regularly, but what is personality? Personality does not have one single definition.

In 1950 Raymond Cattell stated that personality is what allows us to predict what someone is going to do in any given situation.

In 1999 Walter Mischel described personality as the pattern of a person's behavior, which includes their thoughts, their feelings, their actions, and their emotions.

There are many other definitions of personality out there, but one thing that all of them have in common is the idea that a person's personality is made up of the constant behavior that they display. For example, if you are pleasant all of the time, people will describe you as having a pleasant personality.

Every day, we assess different types of personalities. Personality Psychology does this as well; it is the scientific study of what makes you, you. Personality Psychology is about understanding how a person's personality develops, as well as how their personality influences them as a person.

The personality is something that comes from within you. Of course, personality can be influenced by genetics, the environment in which a person grows up, and their life experiences.

The most widely accepted theory of personality is the "Big Five." According to the Big Five Theory, every person's personality is made up of five traits which include:

Extraversion, or how socially confident you are.

Agreeableness, or enjoyable pleasance.

Neuroticism and mental health.

Conscientiousness, which means how well a person wants to do something, or how seriously they take their obligations.

Openness or frankness.

Each trait is one factor of the spectrum, and according to this theory, every personality can be found within that spectrum. An example of this may be that you fall high on the spectrum in conscientiousness and agreeableness, while being in the middle in extroversion and openness, and being low in neuroticism. Every personality can be categorized by using these traits.

Freud believed that personality is developed at a very young age. According to his theory, certain stages need to be gone through for the personality to develop. As a person successfully completes one stage, they move on to the next. However, if the stage was not completed, that would affect their personality for the rest of their lives.

On the other hand, Erik Erikson believed that if a person completed all of the stages of personality development, they would form a healthy personality. While Freud believed that once your personality was developed, you were stuck with it, Erikson believed that it would continue to develop throughout your lifetime.

Have you ever taken a personality test? There are many different types of personality tests out there, and chances are that you have come across one or two in your lifetime. Many of us have taken personality tests when we are applying for jobs. Perhaps you took one when you were in high school, to determine what type of job you should do in the future. Or maybe you took them online as a form of entertainment.

Learning more about your personality is going to allow you to understand why you do the things that you do, why you feel certain ways, and why you work better with some people than others.

If you are taking online personality tests, bear in mind that some of these tests can help you learn a little bit about yourself, and they are fun to do; however, you should not rely on them for any type of diagnosis. If you think that you or someone that you know is suffering from a personality disorder, a formal diagnosis should be made by a personality psychologist.

A personality disorder is a mental disorder that impacts your thoughts, your interpersonal functioning, and your behaviors. At the time of this writing, there are ten personality disorders, including antisocial personality disorder, obsessive-compulsive personality disorder, narcissistic personality disorder, and more.

Being told that you have a personality disorder can be very upsetting, but there is help available for those that want it. When you work with a mental health professional, you are going to begin to understand the difficulties that personality disorders can cause for you, and you are going to start learning coping skills.

The majority of us strive to be good people. However, we find that the world that we live in seems obsessed with learning about those who don't. Psychopaths and narcissists are all the rage. People watch movies and television shows about them, and they seem to fascinate many people.

People like narcissists and psychopaths rank high on the dark triad spectrum. The dark triad spectrum consists of negative traits that any person may possess. Those include Machiavellianism, which means manipulating other people; narcissism, which means that they expect special treatment or admiration; and psychopathy, which means that they are insensitive or callous.

It is this dark triad that constitutes the dark parts of our personality. On the other end of the spectrum is the light triad, comprised of traits that are in contrast to those of the dark triad. These include humanism, or valuing each person and their dignity; Kantianism, which means that you do not set out to use a person; and faith in humanity, which simply means that you believe people are inherently good.

When a person scores high on the dark triad, they generally are unsatisfied with their life, and may display some psycho-social behaviors such as violence, aggression, or low empathy. Those that score higher on the light triad tend to be happier in life, more successful, adept at getting along with other people, and contributing to society.

In all of us exists some light and some dark. Not one single person is going to be all light or all dark. We have to be careful of those that are more dark than light. They are the ones that will exploit, dominate, or abuse you.

While it is the job of personality psychologists to research and understand personality, it is good for everyone to understand a little bit about it. Understanding personality is going to help you better understand yourself, as well as those around you.

Chapter Two: What Narcissism Is and How to Identify It

Narcissism is characterized by an exaggerated sense of self-worth and a lack of empathy for other people. The narcissist lacks empathy, displays arrogant behavior, and has a deep need for an excessive amount of attention from other people.

While these are the most common traits of narcissism, there are so many traits that identifying narcissism can be quite complicated. There is no medical test that can be taken to determine if a person is narcissistic; psychologists must observe the behavior of people, their attitudes, and the way that they react to certain situations.

For a person to be identified as narcissistic, they must exhibit at least 55% of the following characteristics:

> • **Feeling that they are superior to everyone else and having a sense of entitlement.**
>
> The narcissist is only going to be happy when they are identified as the best, the smartest, the most competent, and the one in control. They want everything to be done their way and believe that their way is the best way. What many people fail to realize is that a narcissist can also get that feeling of

superiority from being the sickest, the most injured, the victim, the most upset, the one that has been most wronged, or the one that is the worst off in life. This allows them to enjoy basking in the concern of other people.

- **Having a constant need for validation as well as attention.**

The narcissist needs attention constantly. They may follow you around the house as you are trying to do your chores, demanding your attention, or they may say something off the wall as a means of grabbing your attention. They want everyone to focus on them as much as possible. When it comes to validation, a narcissistic person cannot get this from themselves; they have to have it from other people. You can spend all of your time telling them how much you care about them, how proud of them that you are, and that you really admire them, but that will never be enough. They must have a constant stream of this validation. This is because while they are very self-absorbed and seem like they are extremely secure, deep down, they are actually insecure and feel as if they are not as good as other people. They need constant praise to feed their egos so that they do not feel like they are not measuring up.

- **Perfectionism.**

The narcissistic person has a deep desire for everything everywhere to be perfect. They expect themselves to be perfect as well as you, any event that happens in their lives, their finances, and every other detail in their lives. We all know that perfectionism is impossible, except for the narcissist. They put these high demands on themselves as well as those around them every day. When they or the people around them do not measure up, they are left feeling miserable and dissatisfied with life. This will lead to them complaining about their life or the people in it.

- **Needing to control everything.**

Narcissists are perfectionists - they want to be in control of everything in their lives. They believe that they are smarter than everyone else around them, and by being in control of everything, they will finally be able to be perfect. It is also their sense of entitlement that makes them feel that they should be able to control everything. When they are not in control or things do not work out as they had planned, they become extremely upset, which is why they demand that you do things their way. The only way that things are going to work out the way that they want them to is if you follow their script. In their mind, you are nothing more than a character playing a part in their lives. You do not have your own feelings, thoughts, or ideas.

- **Refusing to take responsibility for their actions.**

They will blame other people. While they want to be in control of everything that happens, they do not want to take any responsibility for the results, unless of course, things work out the way that they want them to. When things don't work out according to their plan, they want to place the blame on you or someone else in their lives because they feel less than perfect, and as we have already learned, a narcissist wants to be perfect. They feel that by blaming someone else for the failure, they are still perfect.

- **Being unreasonable.**

If you have ever known a narcissist, you have probably found yourself trying to reason with them at one point or another. Perhaps you tried to show the narcissist that they were causing you pain with their behavior. Deep down, you want to believe that if they can understand the pain that they are causing you, they will change. To the narcissist, your explanations make no sense. They are unable to accept that you have your own feelings and thoughts. They may tell you that they understand what you are telling them, but the truth is they really don't. The narcissist will continue to make their decisions based off of their own thoughts and feelings. For example, if they want a new car because it makes them feel good when they are driving it, they are going to get it. They are not going to consider the budget. They will not sit down and think about how their decision is going to affect you or the rest of the family. They only think about how that car makes them feel. They spend their time looking for things or people outside of themselves to fulfill a hole within themselves. They expect that everyone else just goes along with whatever they decide to do. If you don't, they can become irrational.

- **Splitting everything into good and bad.**

For a narcissist, anything negative is going to be your fault or the fault of someone else. For example, if they didn't get the promotion at work, it is because no one sees how hard they work. On the other hand, if something positive happens, they will take all of the credit for it. For example, if you worked hard to pay off all of the debt that the two of you had incurred, they may tell people that the debt was paid off because *they* worked so many extra hours.

- **Not being able to weigh the good and the bad of their decisions.**

Similar to the last example, if the narcissist wants to purchase a new car, they are not going to take the monthly payments into account. They are not going to worry about the family not having food on the table because they are focused on the way the car makes them feel.

On the other hand, they may focus completely on the negative. For example, Tom decided that he was going to go to the beach for his vacation. It rained the entire week that he was there. Tom ended up giving the hotel a terrible review because he was so angry about the weather. It did not matter that the hotel did everything within their power to ensure that his stay was a pleasant one. He felt that it was their fault that the vacation was ruined.

- **Having a deep-seated fear of rejection.**

Narcissists are terrified that they are going to be wronged or rejected. They are afraid of being ridiculed, being emotionally hurt, being seen as inadequate, or being abandoned, which is why a narcissist is unable to trust other people. The closer you become to a narcissist, the less they are going to trust you. They refuse to be vulnerable because they know that this will allow you to see their imperfections, leaving them open to your judgment or rejection. Reassurance is not going to help the narcissist at all; narcissists will display worse and worse behaviors in an attempt to see how far they can push someone before they leave.

- **Suffering from anxiety.**

Narcissists feel that something terrible is going to happen to them. They may show this anxiety by talking about the terrible things that they expect to happen, but narcissists hide their anxiety because they are afraid that it will make them vulnerable. Most narcissists are going to project this anxiety onto the people closest to them. They will call them mentally ill, selfish, or unsupportive. They do this so that they do not have to feel the anxiety. As they make you feel worse, they feel better. As your anxiety grows, theirs diminishes.

- **Being unable to feel guilt.**

The narcissist thinks that they are always right. They do not believe that the things that they do affect anyone besides themselves. Deep down, the narcissist may feel a lot of shame; they may understand that there is something wrong with them, even if they are unable to identify it. The narcissist feels ashamed of the fear that they feel, as well as their insecurities. The narcissist will try to hide this guilt in an attempt to hide their low self-esteem.

• Being unable to communicate with others.

While most people are in a relationship or working as part of a team, narcissists think about how their actions will affect the other person or persons. The narcissist never thinks about the other people in their lives. The narcissist will not give up something that they want to provide you with something that you want. They do not believe that you have your own feelings, therefore, they do not consider them.

A narcissist lacks boundaries. They tend to believe that everything and everyone belongs to them. If they are told "No", they become insulted. They behave like toddlers when they want something, going to extremes to get whatever it is they want. They will go as far as pouting, demanding, bugging you persistently about it, getting mad, and refusing to speak to you until they get what they want.

They are unable to empathize with other people. Because the narcissist is so self-absorbed, they rarely consider other people's feelings. A narcissist will rarely apologize for their behavior or feel remorse. They are completely focused on their own feelings and are blind to the way that they make other people feel.

When a narcissist feels that someone is doing something to upset them purposefully, they may react with anger. You may not be trying to upset the narcissist; however, in their mind, that is exactly what you are doing. For example, if the narcissist tries to tell you that the earth is flat and you show them all of the scientific proof that you can find, proving that the earth is round, they will feel that you have deliberately tried to make them look dumb.

They are also known to show off any of the qualities for which they think people will admire them. They want everyone to know how great they are doing at work; if they have done something nice, they will make sure to share it with the world. For example, if they were to give a homeless person a dollar, they would make it sound like they changed that person's life.

They believe that they excel at everything they try to do. Even when they may be having average or below average results, according to them, they are the best in the business.

A narcissistic person will exploit other people and manipulate them. They see people as a means to an end, not as another human that matters. They will do whatever it takes to get what they want from the people in their lives.

Chances are that you have met someone with some of these traits. Many people display at least one of these traits at one point or another in their lives. This is why it is so easy for narcissists to go undetected. It is very simple for a narcissist to come across as a caring person when you first meet them, and that is what makes them so dangerous. Once they pull you in, the red flags start to go up, but you are already emotionally invested. You tell yourself that they are having a bad day or that this is not really who they are. You start to make excuses for them, allowing them to continue to take advantage of you.

By learning about the traits of narcissists, you may be able to protect yourself from being taken advantage of down the road. You may also realize that you have a narcissist in your life already.

Chapter Three: Six Types of Narcissists You Should Know

Today we find that the word narcissist is thrown around fairly haphazardly to describe any person who is highly motivated, self-assured, or knows what they want out of life. The truth is that narcissism goes much deeper than that. Just because a person monopolizes the entire dinner conversation to talk about something that they recently accomplished does not make them a narcissist. A narcissistic person does not just feel that what they have done is important, but that *they* are important. Narcissism is a broad term, though. Within narcissism are several different types, each of them with their own traits and telling behaviors.

Toxic Narcissist - Have you ever known someone who seems to thrive off of causing drama in the lives of other people? Toxic narcissists spend their time causing drama for other people. If you do not meet their demands, they become angry and begin causing issues in your life. They do things like get you fired from a job, try to end your relationships with other people, and can even become physically abusive. (Never allow someone to cause you physical harm. Remove yourself from the situation, seek professional help, and contact local law enforcement to discuss your options.)

Narcissist with Psychopathic Tendencies - Only about 1% of the people in the world is considered psychopathic. However, there is a form of narcissism that comes with psychopathic tendencies. These people are very dangerous and should be avoided no matter what. They are often known for becoming very violent and having no remorse for their actions. When you think about this type of person, you should think about serial killers and other types of murderers as they are the ones that make up the majority of this category.

Closet Narcissists -The closet narcissist can hide their narcissistic traits, making it hard for anyone to identify them as a narcissist. The closet narcissist is still going to feel entitled; they are going to need validation and admiration, but they wear a mask, making themselves look selfless. Think about the person who is always posting on social media about all of the wonderful things they are doing for the world; volunteering at the animal shelter, feeding the homeless, or visiting the elderly. Most people do their good deeds quietly and privately, but the closet narcissist wants everyone to know about them. They want to be admired for all of the good things that they are doing. Most of the time, they don't even care about the people that they are helping; they are only helping so that they will get the attention that they desire.

Exhibitionist Narcissists - This type of narcissist does not care to hide that they are a narcissist. They will let everyone around them know; they are loud, and they are proud. They want to be in the spotlight all of the time, and when they are not, they become very upset. They tend to take advantage of other people seeing them as nothing more than steppingstones to get what they want in life.

Bully Narcissists - This type of narcissist is a self-absorbed bully; they are the people who have to put other people down to build themselves up. They are fixated on being number one and will threaten anyone who gets in their way. A regular bully is one who will bully a person for social or material gain; a bully narcissist will do it because it makes them feel better about who they are.

The Seducer- The seducer narcissist is very tricky. They start by making you feel great about who you are, to win your trust, admiration, or love. Once they have won you over, they will no longer be interested in you. Have you ever known someone who seemed to love the chase, but when they finally obtained the love and admiration of the person they were chasing, they were no longer interested? This is the seducer narcissist. They should be avoided because they can become abusive, and they feel no remorse for the pain that they are causing.

Most of us do not want to have any narcissists in our lives. They are dangerous and should be avoided. They can cause physical, mental, and emotional damage that can take years to repair. To avoid these types of people, you have to be able to identify them. Sadly, this can be a challenge even when you know what you are looking for. If you suspect that someone in your life is a narcissist, and they are displaying narcissistic behavior, the best thing that you can do is remove them from your life. No one has the right to be in your life if you do not want them to be. While the narcissist may react strongly and try to force their way back into your life, you must remain strong and stand your ground to stop them from causing any more harm.

Chapter Four: The Narcissist's Favorite Tools

If you have ever been in any type of relationship with a narcissist, you may have found yourself wondering how you ended up in the situation. You may not understand why you ended up trusting someone so selfish and manipulative.

Narcissists use a variety of tools to take advantage of you, to silence you, and to degrade you. The narcissist does not care if you are in a private or a public place; they will shame you whenever the opportunity arises. They do this to keep your self-esteem as low as possible, to make you feel as if you need their validation, which will keep you hoping that one day you will get their approval, one day you *will* be good enough. That day will never come. They may follow the shaming with "I was just joking" or another phrase like that, but their behavior is inexcusable.

1. When you first meet a narcissist, they can be extremely charming. They tend to sweep you off of your feet when you first meet them and may shower you with compliments. Soon the compliments stop, and the charming personality goes away. The narcissist has trapped you. When you meet a

person that is so charming that they seem to be too good to be true, accept that that is probably indeed the case.

2. The narcissist will always be the victim. If you have had a bad day, they will make sure that you know theirs was worse. No matter what is going on in your life, they are going to make sure that they can top it. Even though their goal is to victimize you, they are going to come across like a victim because it provides them with the attention that they crave. You may start wondering if your problems are really as big as you think they are or if you are just being overly dramatic. The narcissist wants you to feel this way. They want to make sure that you feel that their problems are much bigger than yours because it opens you up to being manipulated by them.

3. Gaslighting is one of the most well-known techniques that a narcissist will use. They do this to make the person question their own sanity. They may tell you that you imagined things that you know you remember, or that you dreamed them. This can cause you to feel as if you are losing your mind, which allows the narcissist to continue to victimize you.

4. A narcissist always wants to be at the top. They want to be in the spotlight all of the time, which means that when you have success in your life or when you achieve anything important, they want to downplay it. They want to make your successes seem less important than theirs. At first, they may complement your success a lot, even to the point that it seems too much. However, as their true colors start to show, they are going to start making you feel that the things you do are just not that good. They do this because it makes you work harder to impress them, which makes them look better and provides them with more attention.

5. Narcissists are known for projecting their shortcomings on to everyone else around them. They refuse to accept that they are not perfect and refuse to take any responsibility for

their own behavior unless, of course, they are getting praised for it. They are never going to focus on self-improvement because, in their eyes, they are perfect. Instead, they will simply project every one of their flaws and all of their bad behavior onto you. One example of this would be that when one spouse is having an affair, they accuse the other person of having one. They are unable to accept their own negative behavior, so they will project it onto their spouse. A lazy employee may claim that they have not been able to be successful at their job because their boss is ineffective. This allows them to maintain their view of themselves while escaping the truth about the situation.

6. Narcissists are great at starting arguments for which you have no idea how it began. You start a conversation with them, thinking that you are going to get to have a thoughtful conversation. Then they start using gaslighting, talking in circles, trying to confuse you and distract you from whatever it was that you were talking about. Disagreeing with them on even the most insignificant topic can lead to a huge argument. For example, if you tell them that the sky is blue instead of the shade of purple that they claim it is, not only is the idea of the sky being blue going to come under attack, but your entire life, every choice you have ever made, and every opinion that you have ever had will come under attack as well. Remember, they tend to thrive on causing drama, and every time that you disagree with them, you are providing them with an opening to cause drama. Don't feed into this. You don't have to prove your point if you know that you are right. Instead, accept that they are wrong and go on with your life. If you see that they are trying to start an argument, cut the conversation short and spend some time taking care of yourself instead of arguing with them.

7. Have you ever had someone misinterpret what you were saying to the point that it seemed absurd that they would come to that conclusion? This is what a narcissist will do. For example, let's say that you are talking to a narcissistic person discussing how you are unhappy with the way someone is treating you. They may respond by saying, "Oh yeah, because you're so perfect," or, "So suddenly I'm the bad guy!", when all you have done is express your feelings about how you are being treated. The narcissist does this to make you feel that you do not have the right to express your own feelings about their or anyone else's behavior. They will try to make you feel guilty about expressing your feelings. They may also claim to know what you are thinking.

Instead of listening to what is being said, they will jump to conclusions about the situation and put words in your mouth. They will say things like, "So you think that I am a bad friend," or, "If you don't want me around, just let me know, and I'll go." This is their preemptive defense. By behaving this way, they make you feel sorry for them, and they ensure that you will not voice your opinion or your feelings in the future. If you react to what they are saying, it is only going to feed into the argument. Instead, simply tell them that you never said that and walk away from the conversation. You are going to show them that you will not be controlled and that you have boundaries that they cannot cross.

1. Moving the goalpost is a technique that many narcissists will use to ensure that they can express how dissatisfied with you they are. They may tell you that they expect one thing, but when you do it, they will say they expected something different. They will criticize everything you do, setting impossible standards and nitpicking instead of helping you to improve. Let's say that you have lost 20 pounds and you are proud of your success. The narcissist will ask why you have not lost 30. If you get a raise at work, they will ask why it was

not more. They do not want you to be proud of any of your accomplishments, so they will make it seem as if you have fallen short. They may even bring up something that has nothing to do with what you were talking about. For example, if you tell them that you got a raise, they may say, "Well, now you can start paying attention to your appearance." They do this to make sure that you are always striving for their approval. When they continually raise their expectations of you, they ensure that you never feel that you are quite good enough for them.

2. Another technique that a narcissist will use is to change the subject to ensure they are not held accountable for their actions. A narcissist does not want to allow anyone to hold them accountable for anything. When they notice that you are starting to hold them accountable, they will change the subject to make themselves look like the victim. They will talk about how they were wronged growing up, how everyone mistreats them, or even go as far as bringing up something that you did years ago that upset them. When this is done, the discussion is derailed, and you do not get to say what you wanted to say. Do not allow them to derail you. If you notice that they are trying to change the subject, switch it back. Become a broken record redirecting the conversation. You can say, "That is not what I was talking about; let's try to focus on this issue." If they refuse, end the conversation and spend your time doing something more productive. There is no point in wasting your time trying to have a conversation with them when they just want to keep changing the subject.

3. A narcissist will use threats when they feel that their sense of superiority is being challenged. They may make very unreasonable demands of you while making sure that you know that you are not living up to their expectations. Instead of talking through a disagreement or behaving maturely, they

will try to make you afraid of any consequences that could happen as a result of you disagreeing with them. They threaten their victims, either covertly or overtly. This should be a red flag, and it should tell you that they will not compromise. These threats should be taken seriously. If you are ever threatened, make sure that the threat is documented and report it to the police immediately.

4. When their sense of superiority is threatened, the narcissist will blow things out of proportion. In their mind, they can't be wrong, and anyone that would suggest otherwise is a threat. When their sense of superiority is threatened, it could result in narcissistic rage. This is not due to their low self-esteem but instead from their extremely high sense of entitlement. Name-calling is a form of narcissistic rage. They use this technique when they are unable to come up with a different way to manipulate you. It allows them to put you down quickly, insult you, and make them feel better about who they are. Instead of focusing on what you are saying, replying to your comments with facts, they will start calling you names in an attempt to make you appear less credible or intelligent. If name-calling begins, end the conversation right away. Do not tolerate anyone calling you names. Remember that you should not take these names to heart, either. They do not represent who you are but who the narcissist is.

5. Further notes on gaslighting (a technique that narcissists use to make their victim question their own sanity): to ensure that the narcissist is not able to use gaslighting on you, you will have to trust your own memories. If you are afraid that you are going to forget details about what happened, write it down. Keep a journal. Write down the date, the time, exactly what happened and what was said. When you bring this with you to any conversation, they are going to be faced with facts, and you will be able to ensure that you are not relying solely on your

memory. When you write things down, you are going to be able to trust that it happened exactly the way that you remember it happening.

6. While many narcissists are very smart, the majority of them are not masterminds; they simply want you to believe that they are. Most narcissists will not take the time to do any research. They will not try to understand any other perspectives but their own. Instead, they are going to generalize everything and make blanket statements that will invalidate any experiences that do not fit into their stereotypes. For example, if there was a news report about a well-known figure making a rape accusation, they may remind you that many rape allegations are false. They may try to make it seem that while falsely reported rape allegations do happen on rare occasions, the majority of rapes are falsely reported.

Or they may make a blanket statement about you, such as, "You are always complaining," or "You always do that." Instead of taking the time to address the specific issue that has upset you, they generalize. The chances are that you might complain now and then, but you don't *always* complain. The chances are higher that the narcissist spends the majority of *their* time complaining and being cruel.

1. A narcissistic person will make sure that you associate memories that should be happy, such as holidays or vacations, with abuse, disrespect, or frustration. They are going to try to ruin every holiday by making it all about them and can even isolate you from the people that you love. They do this to make sure that they are the center of attention. Their goal is to ensure that you are focusing all of your attention on them all of the time. If you can reach your goals and find happiness without depending on them, it threatens their role in your life.

2. When a narcissist is unable to control the way that you feel about yourself, they will take steps to control the way that other people feel about you. They will make it look as if you

are the toxic one in the relationship, and they are the victim. They will do whatever they need to destroy your reputation, ensuring that you have no one to turn to if you decide to cut ties with them. If you are still able to separate yourself from them, they may end up stalking you and claim that they are trying to let everyone know the truth about who you really are.

Not only will a narcissist shame you to your face, but they will gossip about you when you are not around. They will go as far as making up stories about you and claiming to be the victim of the abuse that they are heaping on you.

If this is happening to you, you need to make sure that you are mindful of the way that you react to the narcissist. Always focus on sticking to the facts whenever you have to interact with them. This is especially important if you were married to a narcissist and are going through a divorce. Make sure that you have documentation of any type of harassment. Print out the private messages that they have sent you. Contact law enforcement, when necessary to document the abuse. If you do have to speak to the narcissist, make sure that your lawyer is present.

1. The narcissist is known for belittling the victim. Instead of using sarcasm for fun, they use it to manipulate you. If you say anything about their sarcasm, they may tell you that you are just too sensitive. They tend to forget that they act like a two-year-old whenever they receive negative feedback from anyone. When you are faced with this type of abuse, you will begin questioning your feelings every time you think about voicing your own opinions or talking about your feelings. Suddenly you stop talking about the way that the narcissist makes you feel, and they no longer have to work to keep you silent.

If you find that someone is speaking to you in a demeaning way, speak up. Be firm when you let them know that you are not going to be spoken to like a child and that you are not going to be silent to make them feel better about who they are.

These are just a few of the techniques that narcissists use to control and manipulate their victims. An entire book could be written on this subject alone. Therefore, you need to know what your boundaries are. What type of behavior are you willing to accept, and what type of behavior is unacceptable in any relationship that you are in? Once you know what you will not accept, you will be able to recognize manipulation techniques more easily.

Chapter Five: How Narcissists Choose Their Victims

Have you ever met someone that you felt an instant connection to only to find out that all they wanted to do was manipulate you? Have you ever shared your secrets with someone only to find out that they purposefully collected the information to use it against you later? This is usually how things play out when we meet narcissists.

When you are a compassionate, caring, and trusting person, you want to believe that other people are the same. We all want to believe that people are good. Sadly, this is not always the case. Sometimes we come across people in our lives who only want us in their lives for their own selfish gains.

These people are emotional parasites. They target you, and they take advantage of you. Deep down, you know that something is off in the relationship, but because the narcissist is so good at playing the victim, you feel as if you have to stick it out. After all, everyone else in their life has abandoned them.

Once you have been targeted by a narcissist, you may find yourself wondering why they chose you. You may feel that you are to blame somehow for the way that they have treated you. The truth is that a narcissist's behavior is not your fault. You have done nothing to deserve the treatment that you have received. Narcissists are predators seeking out people on whom they can feed.

When you look back at the relationship, you may realize that you were not the one that started it up; it was the narcissist that initiated it. Realizing that *they* chose *you* may make you wonder, "Why you?" – what was it about you that screamed out to them that they could take advantage of you? There are many things that a narcissist will look for in a victim, including:

> • There is something that you have that the narcissist wants; a specific lifestyle, money, power, or a position.

> • You are a caregiver or someone who has a deep desire to help other people. If this sounds like you be very careful, because you are a beacon to narcissists, one of their favorite types of victims.

> • You are empathetic. If you are an empath, you are the prime candidate for a narcissist.

> • You grew up in a dysfunctional home. If you grew up in an abusive environment, it could make it harder for you to identify abuse in the early stages. It can also make it very hard for you to set boundaries. The narcissist will do whatever it takes to take advantage of this weakness to ensure that you are left completely dependent upon them.

> • You are desperate to find someone to love, or you feel lonely. When you feel lonely or desperate to love, you are going to lower your standards. You just want someone there to fill the void. The narcissist will jump right into position, not to love you but to victimize you.

> • You are okay with accepting blame even when you didn't do anything. If you are the type of person who is willing to accept blame for things that go wrong in your relationships, even when you are not at fault, you will be the perfect victim for a narcissist. They love to place the blame on other people even when it is obvious that they are in the wrong.

- You don't like confrontation and try to avoid conflict at all costs. Narcissists do not want to be in a relationship with someone that is going to confront them about their behavior. Instead, they will seek out someone who avoids conflict because that shows them that they will always be able to take control of any situation in that relationship. They will always get their way.

Before a narcissist chooses their victim, they will test the person. The narcissist will use different techniques to determine if they are going to be able to victimize the person in whom they are interested.

One of the techniques that a narcissist will use is to suggest that you change something about who you are. They may suggest that you change the type of clothes that you wear, the makeup that you wear, your hair, your personality, or your weight. You may be surprised at the suggestion; when you first meet someone and they ask you to change something, such as your hair color or your personality, red flags should go up. Having someone tell you right after meeting you that you need to relax more and let your guard down should scream "narcissist" to you. This is one of the first signs that you are entering a relationship with a narcissist.

When you first meet someone, you do not start telling them all of the things they need to change about themselves. You would never do this to someone, so do not allow anyone to do it to you. Many people fall into this trap, hoping that the relationship has long-term potential when instead, the narcissist just wants to see if you will do what they tell you.

A narcissist will tell you that they are going to call you or come over at a certain time or on a certain day, and then they just don't. You may find yourself completely confused as the days pass and you do not hear from them, only to find them calling or showing up several days later as if nothing happened. They have been out enjoying life and having a blast while you have been at home waiting on them to call you or come over and trying to understand why they haven't.

The narcissist will do this to determine how not calling or coming over has affected you. They are doing this on purpose, even if they have some amazing excuse. I can assure you that this was a test. They may tell you that they had to go out of town suddenly or that they completely forgot to call you. That is not the truth. This test was planned ahead of time to determine how you would react.

Of course, that is not to say that every time this happens you are dealing with a narcissist. If you are in a relationship with someone and this happens one time, the chances are something really did interfere with their plans. If it happens again, though, it is not a mistake. If it happens a second time, you need to recognize that you are dealing with a narcissist. Do not allow them to see that their not calling has bothered you. When they find out that they are not able to affect you, they will go looking for a different victim.

Have you ever met a person who tried to get you to trust them right away? You should be very alert if this happens to you. A person who tells you right after they have met you that you can trust them and that they will not hurt you is likely a narcissist.

This is not to say that you should be on guard 24 hours per day, seven days a week, because there are some great people out in the world. What you do need to be aware of is that trustworthy people do not have to tell someone that they are trustworthy. They are never going to try to convince you to trust them, and they will never try to discuss sensitive topics when they first meet you.

Most of us know that a healthy relationship will progress naturally. In the beginning, you don't want to trust too much, especially if you are still healing from previous relationships. Instead of rushing into things quickly, allow them to progress naturally. One of the biggest mistakes that people make is creating instant relationships with someone they just met. It may seem flattering when someone you just met wants to start an instant relationship, but it should be a red flag.

You may feel excited about all of the attention that you are getting from the narcissist, but deep down, you know that boundaries are being crossed. The narcissist will start violating boundaries as soon as they meet you. They want to find someone that has weak boundaries or no boundaries at all because they know that they are going to be able to enter a relationship with this person and get exactly what they want without having to do anything in return.

Honest people who are trusting and compassionate are the perfect target for a narcissist who is going to start testing boundaries right away. If you do not make your boundaries clear or you don't have any, you will become a target. Many people have a hard time setting boundaries within their relationships. They do not want to cause conflict, nor do they want to be seen as confrontational, which is exactly what a narcissist will look for.

You don't have to have strong boundaries with those that you love; however, when it comes to a person that you have just met, it is important to establish those boundaries right away. This is important because if at some point, you get into a relationship with that person, it is almost impossible to implement boundaries. When you establish them from the start, they are already there.

One thing that you need to remember is that if you have suffered any trauma in your childhood, you can become a target for narcissists. Remind yourself that you are no longer that helpless child. You are a strong and capable adult that can build boundaries and ensure that they are not violated.

Finally, when a narcissist is testing someone to determine if they are going to be their next victim, they will start sharing stories about how bad their childhood was or how terribly their exes treated them. They do this to make you feel sorry for them. Remember when we talked about how the narcissist always plays the victim? This is part of that technique.

The conversation can begin with them asking questions about your childhood or past relationships, but it will end with them oversharing things that have happened to them in the past. It is important to remember that these events may have occurred, but they may have not. The narcissist is not going to have a problem telling you that they were abused, even when they were not, to get you to feel sorry for them so they can take advantage of you.

There is one thing that all of these tests have in common, and it is that they take place right after you have met the narcissist. If you find that someone is oversharing, wanting to know far too much about you too quickly, or is wanting to jump into a very serious relationship very quickly, red flags should go up.

Walking away from a narcissist can be scary at first, but all of the pain that they have made you feel does go away. Seeking professional help when ending a relationship with a narcissist can help you to overcome the damage that they have caused. You can get your life back, though. You can be empowered and independent once again.

Chapter Six: Match Made in Hell: Narcissists and Empaths

An empath is a person that is able to tune into the emotions of those around them. They can tune into the emotions of both people and animals. The empath not only can understand how someone is feeling but many times they will take those emotions into themselves, feeling them as if they were their own.

Empaths are highly sensitive to those around them and may find themselves overwhelmed with emotion when they are in a crowd. They do not only pick up on the emotions of the people that they are talking to, but the emotions of everyone around them.

The trait that most puts an empath in danger around a narcissist is that they are unable to see a person who is hurting, either emotionally or physically, without having the desire to help them. When they see a person in need, they are not able to turn their backs on them. It does not matter how busy the empath is, or how rushed; they will do whatever they can to help someone. This is what makes them so vulnerable.

The empath is the exact opposite of a narcissist, and as you know, opposites tend to attract. Empaths are extremely understanding and filled with compassion, while the narcissist needs someone who is going to praise them constantly. The empath will forgive the narcissist no matter what they do, which will result in the empath being degraded and used while the narcissist thrives in the relationship.

Narcissists will seek out empaths because they know that the empath is going to fulfill every selfish need that they have. The empath is very attracted to the narcissist because they are caregivers, exactly what the narcissist needs.

When a narcissist sees an empath, they see someone who is caring, loving, devoted, and who will bend over backward to make them happy. When the narcissist sets their eyes on a target, they will put up a false front, pretending that they are a loving and compassionate person; as the empath enters the relationship, they are only going to see all of the good qualities of the narcissist, even though the qualities are fake. Of course, the narcissist can only fake it for so long; they will begin pointing out the empath's flaws, while the empath believes that they can help fix the narcissist. The empath's natural instinct tells them that as long as they are compassionate enough, they will be able to heal the narcissist.

They find themselves thinking the relationship would grow fruitful if they only listened more, gave more, tried harder, and on and on. This type of mindset is never going to work when you are in a relationship with a narcissist. Yet the empath is unable to give up on someone; it hurts them to think that they cannot help the person that they love. So, they try harder.

The empath is going to work hard to create harmony within the relationship while the narcissist is going to focus on creating chaos and drama, thereby manipulating the empath. A narcissist will manipulate the empath by making them believe that there is some hope of change. They will provide the empath with little complements or even small acts of kindness which make the empath believe that they have done something right, and if they continue, things will change. Empaths are long-suffering; they understand that we are all just humans and don't expect anyone to be perfect. A narcissist can manipulate an empath by simply telling them, "I'm not perfect. I am trying to change." While the narcissist may admit fault, they do not believe that they are faulty, and they have no intention of making any changes. This is just another technique that they use to manipulate the empath. The empath wants to provide support. They want to help the narcissist grow and become a better person. In the end, the narcissist is just exploiting them.

An empath can look at themselves and recognize their own faults. The narcissist can take advantage of this while forming the trauma bond. The empath will start focusing on the things that they need to change to make the relationship better. The narcissist can point out all of the empath's flaws, and the empath accepts what they are being told.

It can be very difficult for an empath to recognize that they are in a relationship with a narcissist. As an empath, you have to be very careful about the people with whom you form relationships. You have to make sure that you are trying to get them to grow in life but not doing all of the work on your own. You have to take a step back and look at the bigger picture. What steps are *they* taking to make things better?

It is also important to put up boundaries. We talked a little bit about boundaries in the last chapter, but for an empath, boundaries are extremely important. Empaths tend to feel like boundaries are harsh. They have a hard time saying "No" to people. However, that one word can protect an empath from being exploited.

You don't have to become hard-hearted to protect yourself from a narcissist. What you do have to do is accept that not every person is meant to be in your life. You are going to come across people all of the time that are not healthy for you to be in a relationship with, and that is perfectly okay.

If you are an empath and you are in a relationship with a narcissist, you can change the situation by empowering yourself. At first, you are going to notice that the narcissist will push back. They do this because they recognize that the balance of power is starting to shift, and it makes them feel threatened. As an empath, you will need to focus on allowing other people to experience their own emotions and not taking them upon yourself. As the balance of power begins to shift, the narcissist is going to start noticing that you still have a voice. This may make them push back even harder, or they may give up and find another victim.

Understandably, this could be frightening. When you love someone, you want to make them happy. You want to do things for them, and you do not want to do something that is going to make them leave. However, when you are in a relationship with a narcissist, you have to understand that they do not feel the same way about you. You are nothing more than a means to an end for them. You provide them with what they want, and if you are not going to do that any longer, they are going to find someone else to exploit.

We have to be aware that there is a difference between empowering yourself and trying to force the narcissist to change. The narcissist will never change. You, however, can. A narcissist can make you feel as if you will not be able to live without them. They may make you feel that you need them to take care of you and to make decisions for you. They use gaslighting to make you feel as if you are not capable of making decisions on your own. They will attack your self-esteem, putting you down as much as possible in hopes of making you comply with their demands.

If you are in a relationship with a narcissist, you need to make sure that you do not argue with them or try to defend yourself. Simply tell them that you disagree and leave the conversation. Allow the narcissist to deal with their emotions on their own. I know that this can be hard for you, but it is the best way for you to start taking control back from the narcissist.

Chapter Seven: 12 Phrases Narcissists Use (and What to Say Back)

If you have ever been in a relationship with a narcissist - or any type of toxic person for that matter - you probably have a bit of an understanding as to how they use language to manipulate you. They use specific phrases every day that would be used in a completely different text if they were not a narcissist.

Studies have shown that a narcissist enjoys manipulating kindhearted people; they view it as a kind of sport. They believe that they are superior. By manipulating you, they are building on this belief even when all of the evidence points otherwise.

They will use conversations as a way to bring you down or terrorize you. They will cause you to be so afraid to disagree with what they say that you will just give up and agree with them. To understand what a narcissist really means when they are talking to us, we have to decode their language. These phrases below are the most commonly used by narcissists followed by what the narcissist really means.

1. **"I love you."** – I love being able to control you, use you, and own you. I love that I can sweet-talk you, make you believe that I care about you, and toss you to the side as I please. I love that when I flatter you, I can get whatever it is that I want. I love that you have opened up to me even though you were mistreated in the past. I love that I have been able to get you to trust me. I love knowing that I can pull the rug out from under you whenever I want, and watch you crumble.

2. **"I'm sorry."** – I am not sorry. I want this conversation to end so that I can continue enjoying taking advantage of you. I do not care that you were hurt by what I did. I am only sorry that I was caught. I do not like that you are calling me out and trying to hold me accountable for my actions. I do not like dealing with your emotions. They are not valid as far as I am concerned because they interfere with me getting what I want. I do not care how you feel.

3. **"You are overreacting"** *or* **"too sensitive."** – While you may be having a perfectly normal reaction to all of the abuse that I have put you through, I do not like that you are starting to recognize what is going on. I am going to gaslight you to ensure that you continue to second-guess yourself. I need to make sure that you know that your emotions are invalid to ensure that you do not try to stand up to me. I know that if you do not trust yourself, you are going to continue to deny the abuse that I am putting you through. You will rationalize my behavior, blaming yourself for it. While you are busy blaming yourself, you are going to be working very hard to keep me happy. I get all of the benefits without any of the consequences.

4. **"You are going crazy."** – I know that you are not crazy, but I love provoking you and making you think that you are losing your mind. By pointing my finger and saying that you are the crazy one, I can make sure that the focus is taken off of

me and put back onto you. It doesn't matter anyway. I have ensured that no one is going to believe anything that you have to say. They already know how unstable you are. I can make them believe anything about you.

5. **"My ex is crazy."** – My ex really is not crazy, and if he/she is crazy, it is because I made them that way. I had so much fun, torturing, provoking, and agitating them. I was always able to get a reaction out of them, which I used against them to prove to everyone just how crazy they were. Don't worry; I'll tell everyone how crazy you are as well.

6. **"They are just a friend**." – I keep him or her around in case you start to bore me. If I ever get tired of you or if you begin to bore me, they could be your replacement. They are already taking your place when I don't feel like being around you. If you complain about what I am doing, I am going to make sure that everyone believes you are the one that is trying to control me. I will make sure that you seem like the abusive one.

7. **"Stop being so jealous."** – I love making you jealous. I love that you are willing to compete with other people for my attention. It makes me feel so powerful, knowing that I can make you jealous so easily. I can create insecurities within you simply by flirting with another person. The more insecure you feel, the more powerful I feel. Everything that you believe is going on really is, but there is nothing that you can do about it. I am entitled to do whatever I want with whoever I want.

8. **"Your trust issues are not my fault."** – Sure, I know that you should not trust me. I know that I am going to go behind your back whenever I want and do whatever I want, but I'm not going to admit that to you. It would probably be best if you trusted your instincts and got away from me as quickly as possible, but then I wouldn't be having any fun. I enjoy seeing you question your instincts.

9. "It's not always about you." - It's actually never about you. In fact, it is always about me. If you ever decide to start focusing on what you want or need, I will make sure that you feel like the most self-centered person on the planet. I am going to make sure that you feel guilty for even considering taking care of your own needs. I have no desire to fulfill your needs; I couldn't do it if I wanted to. But I don't want to. The focus needs to be on what is important, and that is me.

10. "Can we still be friends?" - I want to keep you around in case I need to manipulate you in the future. I hate to see someone that I worked so hard to train just disappear. I like keeping track of all of my exes. That way, whenever I need some extra reassurance, they are right there for me to start manipulating all over again. Staying friends just makes it easier for me to keep a hold on you. This way, you will never truly be free of me.

11. "No one will ever believe you." - I have made sure that you are completely isolated and have no one to turn to for support. I have destroyed your reputation, making sure that everyone believes every lie that I have ever told about the person that you are. I have made sure that everyone knows that I am the victim in this relationship. If you go looking for help, not one person will believe what you tell them, and they are all still going to think that I am amazing.

12. "You're never going to find another person like me." - It will probably be a really good thing if you never find another person like me. There are people out there who are willing to treat you much better than I ever have. I don't want you to find out that they are out there, though. If you discover your worth, you could leave, and then I have to start all over with another victim. I would rather you just continue trying to make me happy.

Knowing the most common phrases that narcissists use and what they really mean is only half of the battle; it is also important for you to know how to react to what the narcissist is saying. When you know ahead of time how you are going to react to what the narcissist in your life says, you will be able to remain calm and in control. This is going to infuriate them because they are going to begin to see that they do not have control over you any longer. They will recognize that you are starting to take control back from them.

One of the biggest mistakes that people make when they come face to face with a narcissist is trying to get the narcissist to see the logic. You cannot use logic when a narcissist wants to start an argument. They actually enjoy it when you do this because it allows them to use their techniques to make you feel poorly about your views, thoughts, and feelings. Knowing how to respond to them will ensure that you can stop allowing them to take control of these situations.

To do this, you are going to need a few strategies of your own that will help you to stay grounded when the narcissist tries to attack you verbally. These strategies allow you to maintain control of your own emotions even when the narcissist is trying to make you lose control. These five statements can be used whenever you feel that the narcissist is trying to take control from you.

    1. **"Thank you for telling me how you feel."** You can use this phrase whenever you are having a conversation with a narcissist, and they are trying to blame-shift. This shows them that while you have heard what they have said, you are not going to allow it to affect you emotionally. After you have made this statement, you will simply go back to focusing on whatever your point was before they started trying to blame you for the situation.

For example:

Stacy and Todd had been dating for a few months. Stacy needed to talk to Todd about how he flirted with other women

41

when the two of them would go out on dates. When Stacy sat down to have a conversation with Todd, he became angry.

"You're too jealous," his voice boomed as he tried to make her feel bad for her own feelings.

"Thank you for letting me know how you feel," Stacy calmly replied, "I do not appreciate the way that you behave toward other women when we are out together. I deserve more respect than what you are giving me, and your behavior is unacceptable."

As you can see, Stacy did not become defensive as Todd had hoped. Instead, she used her strategy to remain calm and focus on the issue at hand. She refused to allow Todd to control her as he tried to shift the blame to her.

2. **"I wanted you to know how I feel."** We are all tempted to try and ensure that the narcissist knows how we feel; we hope that if they start to understand how they make us feel, they will change their behavior. But they are not going to understand how you feel, nor are they going to care. They know that you want them to understand the damage that they are doing, but as a narcissist, they are going to focus on ensuring you only get the opposite of what you are asking. However, we all need to be able to express ourselves and our feelings. Saying, "I wanted you to know how I feel" allows you to express yourself while maintaining emotional control. Once you have made this statement, you will end the conversation right there.

3. **"Thank you for expressing your opinion."** You can use this phrase when the narcissist goes on and on about a specific thing or when it is obvious that they are just trying to get a reaction out of you. Using this phrase allows the narcissist to express their "feelings" as we all should be able to do, but it also shows them that no matter what their opinions are, you are not going to lose control of your emotions. When you use this phrase, you are not telling them that you agree with their

opinion or telling them that your opinion is wrong. Instead, you are ensuring that you do not feel the desire to have the same opinions as the narcissist. You are never going to have the same opinions as them, no matter how much they try to force you to do so.

4. **"I'm sorry that you feel like that."** You can use this when the narcissist starts using name-calling or tries putting you down.

For example:

Todd knew that he was losing control of Stacy. She had been going out and making new friends, doing things on her own, and he could feel his grip slipping.

"You are the reason that we have so many problems in this relationship," he towered over Stacy as he looked down at her with anger, "If it wasn't for you, we would all be much happier."

"I'm sorry that you feel like that," Stacy calmly replied. She knew that she no longer needed his approval.

You see, Stacy was starting to understand that Todd would do anything to maintain control of the situation. He was trying to convince her that if she tried harder to make him happy, the relationship would be better. Stacy knew that this was just one of the many techniques that Todd used as a narcissist.

When you respond this way to a narcissist's insults, you are not allowing them to affect you. Instead, you recognize that they are trying to insult you, but you also understand that it is what they think, it has nothing to do with who you truly are.

5. **"We have two different opinions on the matter."**

Agreeing that the two of you disagree is going to stop the narcissist from being able to start an argument. This phrase is going to shock the narcissist because they have spent a lot of time training you, making sure that they can make you agree with anything that they say. You may not have even realized up until this point that you have agreed with everything that the narcissist says; you may have found yourself overexplaining your views or opinions, and the reason for this is because deep down, you feel like you need them to approve of what you think. When they don't approve, you simply change your opinions.

Using these phrases allows you to remain calm and think more clearly. When you allow a narcissist to upset you emotionally, you are not able to think clearly about the situation. The narcissist is counting on this happening because they know that if they can keep you from thinking clearly, they will be able to maintain control over you.

A strange thing happens when a narcissist can get you emotionally frustrated. The more frustrated you become, the calmer the narcissist will become. This can make you feel as if you are losing your sanity. On the other hand, when you use these phrases, what you are going to find is that the calmer you are, the more frustrated the narcissist is going to become.

None of these phrases are used to calm the narcissist or make them happy with the way that things are going. These phrases are going to help make you happy, and help you take control of your life away from the narcissist so that you can live your best life.

You should be prepared for the way that the narcissist is going to react when you use these phrases. When you use these phrases, the narcissist is going to realize that they are no longer able to project who they are onto you. This is going to cause them a lot of distress, and they are going to push back.

When you are talking to a narcissist, whether you are in a relationship with them or not, you are going to want to make sure that you let them know that they do not scare you. One of the most common techniques that a narcissist will use is to intimidate their victim. They try to bully you into getting you to do what they want. Ask yourself, "What's the worse that they can do?" Chances are you are going to realize that their worst is much better than what you have been dealing with.

Example:

Todd was at his wit's end. He knew he had to get control of Stacy, but so far, he had been unable to do so. What had suddenly given her this power to stand against him? He knew what she was afraid, of and he knew exactly what he was going to do.

"I came to a decision," Todd walked into the kitchen, returning home from work.

Stacy turned around, looking at him as dinner simmered on the stovetop.

"Really," Stacy raised an eyebrow, wondering what technique he was going to try next.

"I'm going to give it one week," Todd replied, his chest puffed out, "If things don't change, then I'm gone."

Stacy had read about threats. She thought for a moment. What was the worst that could happen? He would leave, find a new victim, and she would be left to start healing from all of the abuse.

"Hmm," Stacy nodded her head as she turned back to the stove.

"What does that mean," Todd's voice was getting louder. Why was she not begging him for a second chance? Why wasn't she upset with his threats?

"I guess if that is what you want, it's your decision to make." Stacy stirred the food, ensuring that it did not burn. She could feel the anger building in Todd as he stood behind her. She refused to react. Sure, she loved him. It broke her heart when she realized that she was nothing more than another victim to him. But she had decided that she was going to be happy in life and she was not going to allow him to take her happiness away from her.

Stacy truly would be better off if Todd would follow through with his threats. Most of the time, this never happens, at least until the narcissist realizes that they have lost all control. The narcissist is not one to give up, though. The majority of the time, it is the victim that must stand strong and end the relationship.

One thing that I do have to mention about threats is that if they are threats of violence or if the narcissist threatens your life, you need to contact the authorities and get help right away. Far too often, people do not take these threats seriously until the narcissist follows through with them. These narcissists are usually narcissistic with psychotic tendencies.

You can use logic when talking to a narcissist, to a point. You are not going to be able to use logic to get them to change their mind about something but using logic to question what they are saying works great.

Example:

Stacy and Todd sat down at the dinner table. Stacy loved to cook and had made a beautiful dinner for the two of them to share. She smiled at her handiwork as she looked down at her plate.

"You know, maybe if you didn't eat so much, you could lose a little weight, and I'd be more attracted to you." Todd was giving it another go. He was going to try his best to maintain control of her.

"You do know that I weigh 105 pounds, which is well within my healthy weight zone?" Stacy smiled as she stuffed a huge forkful of food into her mouth.

What was Todd going to say?

"Well, I think you look fat." he mumbled, scowling at her.

"I'm sorry you feel that way." Stacy replied as she continued to enjoy her meal.

Stacy was able to remain calm as she used logic to block Todd's attacks. He intended to cause her pain, but Stacy made sure that it did not happen. Even if she had not known that Todd wanted to hurt her, knowing that she was at a healthy weight for her height allowed her to block his attack that many people would have been deeply hurt by.

Many times, the narcissist will simply change the subject when the victim responds logically. Remember, you cannot respond logically if you cannot think clearly, and you cannot think clearly if you allow the narcissist to get you worked up emotionally.

You must never allow a narcissist to make a single decision for you. Even something as small as eating a specific meal that they suggest is going to give them a sense of control. Instead, simply say, "Actually, I want this..." while remaining calm. Do what you said you wanted to do and not what the narcissist suggested for you to do.

On the same note, you should never allow a narcissist to order you around. You are not the hired help, and you should not be treated as such. If you find that the narcissist in your life is barking orders at you instead of asking, you could say something like, "Sure, I'd love to if you asked me nicely." When you do this, it is going to not only shock the narcissist, but it is going to force them to change their behavior. Whenever the narcissist starts making demands, simply repeat the phrase and let them know that it is not going to happen unless they learn how to ask politely. If they demand something of you that you do not want to do, simply tell them NO.

Learning how to say no without feeling the need to explain yourself is going to cause the narcissist a lot of distress. Narcissists do not want anyone to tell them no, but when someone does, they expect a really good explanation for it. You, however, do not owe them an explanation when you say no. You shouldn't even try to provide them with one because they usually try to twist what you have said around so that you feel bad. Don't allow them the opportunity to do this.

While nothing is going to stop the narcissist's behavior, using the techniques that you have learned in this chapter are going to allow you to block their behavior from affecting you. What is more important is that they are going to see that you are not going to allow them to victimize you, and while that will drive them crazy, they will usually become bored and go looking for a new victim.

Chapter Eight: Dealing with a Narcissist

Sometimes we have narcissists in our lives that we can walk away from very easily. Sometimes it can be difficult or almost impossible to walk away. Sometimes the narcissist in our lives is a coworker or a family member. Sometimes they are our parents.

While you may not always be able to walk away from every narcissist in your life, you can learn how to deal with a narcissist to bring peace back into your life.

Not all narcissists are abusive. However, if you are in an abusive relationship with a narcissist, these techniques may not work. Instead of trying to deal with the narcissist, you need to start trying to focus on what it is that makes you stay. Why do you continue to subject yourself to the abuse at the hands of the narcissist? It does not matter if it is mental, emotional, or physical, abuse of any kind is abuse, and you do not have to accept being treated that way. Please alert the authorities to what is going on and seek professional help so that you can deal with the damage that has been done. Remember, the abuse that the narcissist has inflicted upon you is not your fault. They are responsible for their actions, and nothing that you could do or say would make it okay for anyone to abuse you.

Before we get into learning how to deal with a narcissist, we have to first start by talking about denial. We can all spot denial when we see it. We see people all the time living in denial, not wanting to face the truth. A narcissist will be in denial about being a narcissist. How far in denial they are at the time will affect how well the techniques that we are going to talk about work. If the narcissist is deep in denial, these techniques may not work as well as they would if there was only a bit of denial.

How can you determine this?

Can the narcissist admit that there is a problem? Something as simple as admitting that their life is not what they expected it to be can provide you with some hope. Many people do not believe that a narcissist can admit that there is a problem, but the truth is that many of them have sought out therapy of some sort to help them understand what is going on. These are vulnerable narcissists, and you can learn how to deal with them.

When you are dealing with a narcissist, you have to be aware of the manipulation. We already know that narcissists are great manipulators, which means that they can convince you that they are changing, that they are interested in changing, or that they know there is a problem... but only if they think that they are going to benefit from doing so. Of course, not all narcissists will take things this far. However, those that are willing to are very dangerous because they can make you believe that they are willing to change and go through all of the motions, completely deceiving you.

You should also determine if they are willing to change. Just because you have a deep desire for them to change does not mean that they have that same desire. The best option would be for them to see a therapist. Are they willing to take that step to change? Most people who want to change are willing to do whatever it takes to see that change come to pass in their lives. Are they?

It is also important for you to take a good look at yourself. Are you extremely angry with them? The narcissist has probably spent a lot of time putting you down or name-calling. They may have openly talked about how attractive they find other people in their lives. It is possible that if you are in a relationship with a narcissist that they have cheated on you. When we are faced with all of this, our natural instinct is to make sure that we are protected from any damage that they would do. Many of us end up wearing full armor whenever we are around that person to ensure that no matter what they say, we do not suffer pain.

Anyone that has had to deal with narcissists in their lives would take measures to protect themselves, and that is completely understandable. The problem with this full suit of armor is that it can stop the narcissist in our lives from seeing the damage that they are doing. They are unable to see how sad you are, that they are causing fear, or that you love them. You have completely detached from them and the situation as a means of protecting yourself.

Can you remove some of that armor and allow the narcissist to know how you feel? If they say something hurtful or demeaning, calmly let them know exactly what they have done and how it made you feel. Start with a positive, "You mean so much to me." Then tell them how you are feeling, "When you say things to me like that, it makes me feel worthless and that you do not care about me at all."

Studies have shown that when people in a relationship learn to express themselves this way, their relationship is repaired far more often than it fails, and it is actually stronger than ever before.

Anger is not the only thing that you have to check, but you also need to understand how you are responding to the narcissist. Are you responding with silence? It is so easy for us to become angered by condescending remarks that a narcissist makes; however, once they have broken you down, their remarks often lead you to shutting down. How often are you shutting down? You may find that you are spending hours on end without saying a single word. If you want things to get better, you are going to have to learn how to speak up. Find your voice.

When a person withdraws into silence, they are using their coping skills to deal with the sadness or fear that the other person has caused them; this is a natural impulse. Sometimes, though, we have to learn how to fight against these natural impulses and speak up about how we are feeling. Speaking out is extremely important because the narcissist is going to take your silence as an acceptance of their behavior or the words that they have said to you. When you tell them how they are making you feel, you will force them to hear the pain that they are causing you, whether they want to take responsibility for it or not.

It is important that you are honest with yourself, as well. If you have tried to open up to the narcissist and if you have tried to explain to them that they are causing you pain, but they refuse to change, you have done everything in your power, and you should accept that.

If you choose to stay in a relationship with the person, it is going to come at a very high price. Be honest with yourself when you ask yourself these two questions:

> 1. Am I staying in this relationship because I feel that they are doing everything within their power to change?

> 2. Am I staying in this relationship because I am afraid that it is going to be too hard for me to leave?

The narcissist may truly want to change, but that does not mean that you have to continue to endure the same pain over and over again. You can remove yourself from the situation and choose to be happy.

Narcissists have a way of getting under our skin. We naturally respond by either pushing back at them or pulling away from them. That is exactly what they want. It is this chaos and drama that they feed off of. When you let them see what they are doing, the damage that they are causing, you are allowing them not only to hear you but to change. If they are unable to understand your pain, the chances are that they never will. It is sad, and it can be very difficult, but you have to take care of yourself, and sometimes this means ending the relationship.

We have options when it comes to dealing with a narcissist. The first option is to remove the person from your life.

In Intimate Relationships

1. Just stop trying to understand them, stop accepting their behavior, stop letting them take advantage of you, and completely cut them out of your life. Most people are going to tell you that the best way for you to deal with a narcissist is to cut them out of your life completely. That may be true for some, but it does not have to be true for all. However, a narcissist is going to do whatever they can to ensure that every moment of your life is dedicated to serving them in some way. No one deserves to live that way.

If you feel as if you are stuck in a relationship with a narcissist, you can end it. You should not feel any shame when it comes to ending a relationship where you have to endure the abuse of a narcissist. No one has the right to abuse you in any way, shape, or form, and you do not have to continue with the relationship.

2. Do not allow the narcissist to violate your boundaries. If they have in the past, it is time for you to build those boundaries back up and make it very clear to them that you will not allow them to violate the boundaries again.

While the best thing that you could do is to remove them from your life, when it is not possible, such as when they are your family, you may decide that you want to distance yourself from them. There are going to be times when you cannot distance yourself from the narcissist. For example, if your boss is the narcissist that you have to deal with, you will not be able to cut them out of your life or distance yourself from them.

You could choose to switch jobs; for now, though, let's assume that you are going to stay at your job.

If your boss is the narcissist that you are dealing with, you are going to have to be able to separate work life from home life. Even if the person is not your boss but just someone that you work with, you need to make sure that you do not let them know anything about your life outside of work. When narcissists at work start learning about our home lives, they begin collecting information about us that they can use against us later. Maintaining your boundaries is going to be worth it because it can save you a lot of headaches down the road.

3. Honesty is the best policy. Narcissists are pros at playing games. Because they are so good at playing these games, you may find yourself tempted to play along with their games. Do not play along! Their behavior will hurt your life or your job. If they are behaving unacceptably, make sure that you let them know. If it is possible, walk away from the situation. If the narcissist is your boss or is someone that you work with, let them know that their behavior is not acceptable then turn the focus back on to whatever it is that you needed from them in the first place.

When you call them out and let them know that their behavior is not acceptable, you will not change what they do or the fact that they are a narcissist, but it will reduce the negativity when you do have to interact with them.

4. When you assess the situation, make sure that you are honest with yourself about what is really going on. Everyone behaves selfishly on occasion, but not everyone is selfish. When a person is a narcissist, they do not behave selfishly on occasion, but they are selfish people. You should never just assume that someone is a narcissist simply because they have behaved selfishly once or twice. Remember, the person could simply be having a terrible day, or they may have just gotten

out of a terrible relationship where they were abused, and they have decided to take some time to put themselves first.

5. Refuse to engage in the narcissist's drama. Narcissists are emotional vampires. For them to feed, they have to cause drama. Never react to their behavior no matter how much it escalates. Never give any attention to their behavior. The more attention that you give to their behavior, the more it will escalate. They will do whatever they can to ensure that you are taking care of them. Once they have sucked you dry, they are going to toss you to the side and find a new victim to feed off of. They are going to do everything within their power to make you believe that everything bad that happens is completely your fault. Being blamed can cause you to lose your cool if you wear your heart on your sleeve.

When you react to a narcissist's behavior, you are communicating to them that you will tolerate their behavior. Everyone has a bad day now and then, and everyone will need support from their friends from time to time. However, when someone has a bad day every day and needs constant support from you, the relationship could be toxic. If the person has narcissistic traits and is constantly asking for your support, you need to protect yourself and make sure that you are not engaging in their drama.

6. Respond politely to the narcissist. Passive aggressiveness is not usually something that is recommended, but when you are dealing with a narcissist, this could be your best option. When they start calling you names, putting you down and then acting as if they are doing you a favor by letting you know all of your flaws, all you have to do is smile and tell them, "Thank you." Or tell them that you appreciate their advice. Even though you do not appreciate what they are saying to you, what you are showing them is that you are not going to allow their words to upset you or your life. A narcissist uses name-calling

and put-downs as a way to make you feel inferior to them. It increases their sense of superiority, and if they get a dramatic reaction from you, they can feed off of the negativity. When you politely respond to them, they will become bored with you and start looking for another victim.

In Family Relationships

Being in an intimate relationship with a narcissist is one thing, but when they are part of your family, it is something else altogether. You have been exposed to their behavior all of your life, and you have no way of removing them from your life. However, there are things that you can do to help you deal with the narcissist to whom you are related.

1. Accept that they are a narcissist and move on with your life. You have to accept the fact that you are not going to be able to fix or cure the narcissist. The narcissist is never going to become the person that you hope they will. They are only going to continue causing you pain. Distancing yourself from the person is the best place to start. This will allow you to understand that you cannot change them.

2. You may want to call them out and tell them that they are a narcissist, but the chances are that this will backfire and only make things worse than what they are. When you tell someone that they are a narcissist, you are probably doing it to try to make them stop what they are doing. However, a narcissist is not able to reflect upon their behavior. Instead of stopping what they are doing, they are going to decide that their goal is to prove you wrong. They are going to become convinced that you are the person that has the problem. Telling someone that they are a narcissist is going to cause problems within your relationship, and it can give them even more of a reason to make your life miserable. They are not going to stop until you apologize for what you have said and admit that you are the one with the problem.

3. Narcissistic people tend to feel that the entire world has done them wrong. They believe that everyone treats them unfairly. They also believe that they are not being given the respect that they deserve. The narcissist cannot see how their behavior causes people to avoid them or to criticize them. If you have a family member who is always complaining about how hard their life is and how they never get a fair chance, don't feed into their negativity. Instead, tell them, "I hate that you feel that way. Maybe you should put your energy into something else. You always have a choice in life." You can end by telling them good luck.

Doing this may also help you to remember that you have choices in life as well. You can choose to distance yourself from the narcissist or limit the amount of time that you spend together. If you can't distance yourself, a good idea would be to bring another person along when you have to be around the narcissist. Having a third person to witness their behavior usually helps to reduce the behavior.

4. Find someone to support you. Most of the time, when a person is dealing with a narcissistic person, their self-esteem begins to crumble due to all of the criticism, humiliation, and insults. When you have suffered so much abuse, you are going to need some extra support. You can get this from going to therapy, from other members of your family, and from your friends. Be open about your experiences; you should never be ashamed of falling victim to a narcissist.

In the Workplace

The above techniques are all great techniques to use if you are in a relationship with a narcissist or if you are related to a narcissist. But most of them are not going to be of much help if you work with the narcissist or if the narcissist is your boss. Don't worry; there are things that you can do to deal with a narcissist in the workplace.

• Make sure that you get everything in writing when you are dealing with a narcissist at work. If they try to give you instructions verbally, request that they email you the instructions. Make sure that you can document everything possible. You can ask them to send it to you in an email "so you don't forget". You can print these documents out, making sure that you include the time and date that you received them. If they begin causing problems at work or claiming that they told you to do one thing when they actually told you to do something else, you will have documentation to prove what really happened.

• Do not ever fight with them. Avoid fighting as much as possible when you are at work. A narcissist at work is going to do whatever they can to cause you problems, and that could include getting you fired. Do not allow them to cause problems for you. A narcissist is going to seek out your weakness and exploit it. They will find anything that you are sensitive about and use it against you. For example, if they have seen a picture of your children sitting on your desk, and you make them angry, they may make sure that you hear them having a conversation about how terrible a parent you are. They know that when they start questioning the things that you love in life or your most important roles, you will react. They will use that reaction to start causing problems for you.

• Remind yourself that the attack is not personal. It may seem very personal when a person at work is attacking you but remember that a narcissist will attack anyone at work when they perceive that person as better than they are. They are attacking because of their own personal insecurities. When you know this, it can make it easier for you to walk away from the drama that they are trying to cause.

• The narcissist may come to you and tell you that they want to talk to you in private. If they do this, you need to make sure that you do not allow it to happen. Make sure that you bring a witness with you. This will help ensure that the narcissist thinks twice about what they plan on saying to you and abusing you. When you have a witness, it also means that while the narcissist may try to go to your superior and tell them lies, you will have someone that will be able to back up your version of events.

• Avoid contact with the person as much as possible. Avoidance can be the hardest of all of the techniques. However, it is the best one to use if you want to ensure that you do not get caught up in their games. If you do have to interact with the person while you are at work, make sure that you stick to the facts. Get exactly what you need from them or provide them with what they need and end the interaction as quickly as possible.

• You can talk to your boss about the narcissist if they are someone that you have to work with regularly, or you can pay a visit to human resources. Some people may go as far as requesting a transfer due to the abuse that they suffer at the hands of a narcissist at work. You do not have to allow this behavior to continue. You may find that there have been other reports made about this person, or you could find that you are the first. If you find that you are the first person to make a report about the narcissist abusing you, it is probably because they have everyone else too scared to speak up. Be that voice that is needed to tell the narcissist that their behavior is not okay.

• Do not let the narcissist have the satisfaction of knowing that they are getting to you. Do not react to their abuse or try to lash out at them in retaliation. If the narcissist thinks that they are not causing you pain or drama in your life, they will likely move on to the next victim. If they can see that they are causing problems for you at work or home, they are going to continue with their behavior. When a narcissist cannot get a response from someone, they quickly become bored with that person and are forced to find a different target. Remind yourself that you did nothing to warrant this type of abuse, and you do not have to allow it to affect you.

Remember that harassment of any form is a violation of your rights as an employee, even if the person harassing you is your boss. You can visit the EEOC website if you need to get into contact with labor attorneys to discuss your case.

Before you decide to talk to a labor attorney, you may want to consider following the chain of command. If the person who is harassing you is your boss, consider talking to their boss. Report the harassment, ensuring that you have documentation to back up your claims, as well as witnesses. Remember, it is the goal of the narcissist to make you dislike your job so much that you leave it. They feel threatened by your presence in the workplace, and they are doing everything within their power to remove that threat. Do not allow them that satisfaction. Do not allow them to be successful.

While it would be wonderful if we could avoid narcissists, not all of us can. You may be related to the narcissist, or in a relationship with them or you may work with them. By using the techniques that we have gone over in this chapter, you can reduce the damage that the narcissist does in your life. You can take control back from the narcissist.

If you have been the victim of a narcissist in the workplace, you should consider talking to a therapist. Being the victim of any type of abuse is damaging, and it is beneficial to have someone on your side who knows how to help you recover.

Chapter Nine: Why We Love Narcissists (and How to Stop Falling for Them!)

You know that narcissists are toxic. You know that they are arrogant, self-centered, and manipulative. Yet you continue to keep falling in love with them. Studies have shown that even though we know the narcissist is bad for us, we are attracted to their personality, the fact that they can take control of any situation, and we can even be attracted to their hostility.

When we look at a narcissist, we see someone who is strong and outspoken; we see them as someone charming, interesting, and the life of the party. Of course, that is what they want us to see when we first meet them.

Narcissists are extremely popular, much more than other people. Their sense of authority is highly appreciated. They are seen as leaders by those around them. The tone of voice that they use can attract you to them, as well as the way they have mastered their facial movements, and you will usually find yourself attracted to their physical appearance.

When you first meet a narcissist, you will most likely be drawn to their ability to use facial expressions to appear extremely confident. It is not only their facial expressions that screams confidence to us, but it is also the clothes that they wear, their haircut, and their fun personality.

Of course, these assumptions are made off of the first impressions that the narcissist gives off. Later, when we get to know them better, they show us who they really are. The narcissist will cover up their tendencies when you first meet them to draw you in and gain your trust.

Narcissists can thrive in the dating environment because they care about how they look. Of course, we know that a narcissist will care far too much about how they look, but when you first start dating someone, you find this attractive. A person's physical appearance has a huge impact on whether we choose to date them. We live in a world where appearance is very important. Even simple pictures that are posted on social media have to be cropped, and filters added before we will allow the world to see them. Because we find physical appearance so important, we tend to be more attracted to people who focus a lot on their physical appearance.

Narcissists are very good at selling themselves. They know how to make people look up to them and how to make themselves look good. You may also find that you are attracted to them because of their confidence. While we already know that this confidence is nothing more than a mask that the narcissist wears, it can be hard to determine whether it is real or fake at the beginning of the relationship.

Every day narcissists start their morning by looking in the mirror and telling themselves how wonderful they are. All of that practice has allowed them to convince themselves that they are the best, so it makes it very easy for them to convince you of the same thing.

These are only minor traits when it comes to the main reason that a narcissist does so well in the dating field. Being an extrovert and focusing on physical appearance is great, but the thing that narcissists do that draws most people in is their flattery. By providing their potential victim with compliments, gifts, and attention, it looks as if they are enamored of them. When a person comes across as trying to create a healthy relationship, they can gain the trust of the person they are dating.

Sadly, what is happening most of the time is that they are just probing you for information. It may seem as if they are trying to learn as much about you as they can; they are. They are trying to learn everything they can about you. However, they are doing it so that they can use it against you later.

You can start asking them questions, shifting the focus on to them, which is going to slow them down when it comes to collecting information about you, and it is going to allow you to determine whether or not the person that you are seeing is a narcissist. If you tell them, for example, that you love to go hiking and they tell you that they do as well, you can start asking questions about where they like to go hiking, why they enjoy it and so on. Try to make your questions as detailed as possible because this is how you will find out if they are lying.

It is very easy for someone to tell you that they like the same things that you do, but when you start asking them about it, you may find out that they are not as interested as they pretended or that they know nothing about it at all. What many people find when they start asking narcissists questions is that the narcissist is caught off guard and suddenly less attracted to them.

When you are in a relationship, it is just as important for you to get to know the person that you are seeing as it is for them to get to know you. Asking them questions should not be something that makes them turn away from you unless they have a hidden agenda.

As you move into a relationship with a person or as you start dating them, you want to make sure that you do not tell them anything about yourself that you would not tell your boss. People tend to overshare early on in the relationship, but as you already know, the narcissist is focused on gathering as much information about you as they can so that they can use it against you later. Not only can this information be used against you, but it is going to provide the narcissist with a sense of intimacy that does not exist between the two of you.

In a relationship, we share personal information about ourselves in an attempt to become close to other people. A narcissist will use this technique to get very close to you very quickly. Generally speaking, it is never a good idea for two people to become very close very quickly. The narcissist will start sharing what we would consider private information because they know there is a natural urge within us to share information that is on the same level as what has been shared with us. They know that when they open up to us, we may end up opening up to them as well, providing them with information that they can hold over our heads later.

Have you ever met someone, gone on a date or two, and suddenly found yourself in a relationship not quite understanding how it happened? That is what a narcissist will do. They will jump right into a relationship from the very start. If they tell you that they are worried that you are going to break up with them or that you are not going to stick around, the red flags should start going up. The narcissist will use this technique to gain reassurance from you. They want to know that you are too desperate to leave the relationship, even if it is a bad one.

They may tell you that they have to leave town soon, in an attempt to find out if you are willing to commute or even move to where they are going to be relocating. Remind yourself that you are not in a serious relationship with this person. The relationship is in its early stages and does not warrant any type of commitment to the person. Narcissists are great at isolating people, and this could be exactly what they are trying to do. By getting you to move to a new town, they are ensuring that you have no one to turn to and that you are stuck with them. Do not allow the other person to rush you when it comes to the pace of the relationship. Make it clear that you are going to move at a pace that you are comfortable with.

Narcissists are notorious for love bombing, which means that they pour a huge amount of love out on you to get you to do what they want you to do. The narcissist is great at making you feel that they are taking care of you. They will make you feel that they adore you, but the truth is that what they are doing has nothing to do with how much they love you. Instead, it has to do with the narcissist getting what they want out of you by using techniques that they know will work.

If you suspect that the person you are in a relationship with is using love bombing, start paying attention to what they are getting out of the situation. Tell them that you would like for them to slow down and that the relationship is moving too fast for you. Let them know that you want to take the time to get to know each other before plans for the future or any promises are made.

See how the other person reacts. If they respect your wishes, the chances are that they really are a good person and are just very enthusiastic about the relationship. On the other hand, if they are a narcissist, they will continue to use love bombing to get what they want from you.

If the other person does not stop, if they continue to move at a pace that you are not comfortable with, be very firm and tell them to stop. Then get away from them. Don't go back to them just because they promise you that they will slow down. I promise you they will not.

Don't allow yourself to be caught up in some fantasy; the narcissist may look like Prince Charming, but he is nothing more than a heartbreaker.

Another technique that a narcissist will use when you are dating them or in a relationship with them is that they will want to occupy all of your time. They will want you focused completely on them. Have an hour-long lunch break at work? They'll show up. Are you spending the evening at home focusing on self-care? They'll call multiple times to find out what you are doing, even asking if you have other people there with you. Want to go out with your friends for the evening? The narcissist will throw a fit, try to start a fight, and even show up to surprise you. They will do whatever they can to keep you from spending time with your friends and your family.

That is not enough for the narcissist, though. They do not want any of your attention focused anywhere but on them. Have hobbies? When you get into a relationship with a narcissist, you won't have them any longer. Want to pursue your interests? When you are in a relationship with a narcissist, you don't have time to focus on your own interests because you are too busy making sure that they are happy.

How can you tell if the person you are dating is a narcissist? Tell them that you are going to the movie with your friends. They will start asking all sorts of questions. What friends are you going with? What movie are you going to see? What theatre are you going to? (chances are they will show up with or without you knowing). What are you doing after the movie? Turn your phone off and watch them lose their minds. It is likely that when the movie is over, and you turn your phone back on, the notifications from them will go crazy.

Don't answer all of the questions that they ask. Instead, be vague. "Oh, we haven't decided on what movie yet. What theatre? Hmm, I forget which one they said we are going to. Which friends? Oh, just some old friends I've known forever, you don't know them." See how that works? You have let them know that you have heard their question, but you have also shown them that you are not going to answer them. This will make a narcissist lose their minds, and they will not want to be in any type of relationship with you.

The narcissist wants you all to themselves. When the narcissist can separate you from all of the people that you care about, they can start controlling you. Having even one person in your life that cares about you and that you can turn to makes it very hard for the narcissist to take control of you. If you are in a healthy, loving relationship, your partner is going to want you to have friends and hobbies of your own. They are going to want you to do things that make you happy.

Narcissists love to move quickly, and they may try to move in with you right away. If they know that you are not going to let them move in, they may start talking about "sleepovers" very early on in the relationship. This should be a huge bright red flag.

If you are on a date very early on in the relationship and the other person starts talking about sleeping over at your place that night, simply say something like, "Oh sorry, I have plans with my friends after our date." Let them know that they cannot stay at your place. This is very important for you to do. A narcissist knows that if they can get you to live with them, they will be able to take control of your entire life.

When two people move in together too quickly, there is no balance in the relationship. You go from being single to feeling as if you are stuck with this person for the rest of your life. There is no time for the relationship to grow; this is not natural. Humans do not want to spend all of their time alone, which is why we have marriage in the first place. However, when you jump into a serious relationship spending all of your time together too quickly, you are not allowing the relationship to grow naturally.

One of the reasons that so many people move in with someone too quickly is because they have a deep need to be a caretaker. Resist that need to start taking care of that person you do not really know. If you have just met someone or you have just started a new relationship with them, it is not your job to take care of them.

Understandably, you may feel the desire to do so. The narcissist may play off of your sympathy. They might tell you that they recently lost their job; they are out of money and are not going to have a place to live, or that they don't have anywhere to go since they ended their relationship with their ex. They may tell you that their family refuses to help them out, and they have no one to turn to.

If the person tells you that they just left a terrible relationship and they don't have anyone to turn to, let them know that you will not be anyone's rebound and move on with your life. You do not want to risk getting hurt by being the rebound. If they tell you that their family will not help them out, ask yourself why. Maybe their family knows something about them that you do not.

Stop fighting against your instincts. If your gut says that something is wrong, it is probably wrong. It is natural for us to want to help the downtrodden. We want to pick up the injured and nurse them back to health. We want to help make people whole again. However, this is not how healthy romantic relationships are created. A romantic relationship should be between two adults who are self-sufficient and can take care of themselves on their own. If the person that you are dating is not able to support themselves, the chances are that they are not going to be able to pull their weight in the relationship. They are instead going to take advantage of you and push all of the responsibility off on you.

Everyone likes to dream about the future and make big plans, but if you have just met someone or are just starting a relationship with someone and they are already talking about the future or about being together for the rest of your lives, you need to put the brakes on.

Stating, "We're getting a little ahead of ourselves here," is a good way to do this. If they start talking about moving away, getting a house together, or spending your lives together early on in the relationship, use this phrase to let them know that you are not comfortable talking about these things with them. They need to understand that they are not going to push you into something that you are not ready for.

The goal when you are dating is to find someone that you can have a long-term relationship with, but that does not mean that you have to start making these plans right from the beginning. If you do, the narcissist is going to use this against you later on when you want to end the relationship. "This is what you wanted. I gave you exactly what you ask for, and now you are quitting on us."

When you are out on a date, watch how they treat other people. Does your date spend the entire evening belittling the staff at the restaurant? Do they embarrass the waitress or seem to enjoy making other people feel poorly about themselves? How would you feel if the person you are on a date with treated you the way that they treat the people around you? If they tend to treat other people in a way that makes them feel less important, I can assure you that they are going to do the same thing to you at some point in the relationship.

Find someone kind to other people. Pay attention to how the person that you are with treats waitresses or cashiers. If they are respectful and kind to these people, they are probably a good person, and they will be respectful and kind to you as well.

Meeting a narcissist, being love-bombed, and falling victim to them can happen so quickly that many people do not even notice that it is happening. However, by using these techniques, you can be aware of the very start of the relationship just what kind of person you are dating.

You are going to protect yourself from any abuse or pain at the hands of a narcissist in the future. You are going to be able to ensure that you do not fall victim to a narcissist ever again, and that is great news. The bad news is that while you may like the way that a person portrays themselves, you may find out that they are actually a narcissist, trying to take advantage of you, and you will end up having to walk away from the relationship.

While this is no fun, it is much better than becoming the victim of an abusive narcissist.

Chapter Ten: A Narcissist's Secret Fears

Narcissists put a lot of effort into making others believe that they are very confident and successful. The narcissist may act like they are superior to everyone else. They will boast about how great they are and thrive on the attention that they get. They believe that they are special because only the most important people get this type of attention. The narcissist does not believe that anyone else deserves the type of attention that they get. Ordinary people simply are not worthy of it. To the narcissist being special means that they are not ordinary. They are not like everyone else.

Deep down, the narcissist is actually very fragile. They have fears that they try to hide from everyone around them. By knowing these fears, you can use them against the narcissist to ensure that you do not become their next victim. If you are already the victim of a narcissist, you can use those fears to make them lose interest in you.

1. The narcissist has flaws. Narcissists believe that they are perfect, and they want everyone else to believe that as well. This is why when something negative happens, they will blame it on other people. They do not want anyone to perceive them as anything but perfect. If they were not perfect, they would

not be special, and they do not want to be known as ordinary. The narcissist will not want to admit that because they are human, they will make mistakes and have imperfections. They do not want to admit to experiencing self-doubt because this could make them seem weak.

A narcissist will become offended by simple truths that affect all humans, such as everyone has limitations, everyone suffers loss at some point in their lives, no one can do everything on their own, everyone has flaws, and no one is perfect. The narcissist is constantly on guard, making sure that they are ready for anything that could happen to make them look less than perfect. They will do everything possible to ensure that no one sees their flaws.

While this may sound like an exhausting task, the narcissist will simply project every flaw that they have onto the people around them. What is ironic about this situation is that a person who is what the narcissist would define as superior would never need to build themselves up by putting other people down.

Knowing that the narcissist is terrified of their flaws being revealed can be very freeing. Knowing what they are afraid of can help you to understand why their rage has been triggered.

2. Narcissists are terrified of being in a real relationship. This is not to say that a narcissist will not be in any relationship but that they will not commit themselves to a relationship. You have already learned that a narcissist will not let their guard down. When you enter a real relationship, or when you choose to be committed to a relationship, letting your guard down is a necessity. Being in a committed relationship means that you have to let the other person see who you really are. A narcissist cannot do this.

A narcissist knows that if they allow someone to get too close to them, their insecurities will be exposed. They know that the person that they are in a relationship with is going to learn all of their secrets, and a narcissist cannot allow that to happen.

3. Self-reflection is a very important part of self-improvement, but this is something that a narcissist cannot take part in. The narcissist is in denial about who they really are, and one of their biggest fears is having to face that. The narcissist wants to believe that they are perfect, but they know that if they practice self-reflection, they are going to have to face their flaws, insecurities, and other issues that they do not want to deal with.

4. While a narcissist can dish out insults one right after the other, they are unable to handle being insulted. Narcissists can spend all day criticizing other people, but when this criticism is turned back on them, they cannot handle it. The majority of narcissists do not have as much confidence and self-esteem as they want you to believe. In fact, their egos are very fragile. Because of this, when they are insulted, it devastates them and takes a huge toll on their already low self-confidence.

5. A narcissist does not experience guilt when they hurt another person; therefore, this is not a concern for them, but what they are afraid of is shame. The shame that the narcissist is afraid of is the feeling of being unworthy.

6. One of the biggest fears that a narcissist will have is a lack of admiration. A narcissist is much like a performer. They want the spotlight to be on them all of the time, but more than that, they want everyone to admire them. They are willing to go to great lengths to get the admiration of other people. The narcissist is going to take extreme measures to impress other people, and they fear that those attempts will be ignored.

7. A narcissist fears being exposed for what and who they truly are. Narcissists tell lies all of the time. They may end up telling so many lies that they are unable to keep up with them

all. They may lie about past relationships, experiences that they have had in life, their family, childhood, or their accomplishments. They use these lies to impress the people around them or to manipulate their victims into doing what they want them to do. The narcissist knows that by telling these lies, they are going to be able to get what they want from the people around them but deep down, they are terrified that they are going to be exposed. They are afraid that people will begin to compare notes about them, and that they will be called out on the lies that they have told. They are afraid that people will learn the truth about them.

8. To a narcissist, expressing gratitude means that they were dependent upon another person. Because the narcissist does not want anyone to think that they need them, they are unable to express gratitude. Saying thank you is almost impossible for a narcissist to do. They do not want anyone to know that they need help, and they refuse to admit that they do. Showing gratitude, even by saying "thank you", goes against everything that a narcissist is.

9. The narcissist fears death. The narcissist thinks of themselves as untouchable. In their opinion, nothing bad could ever happen to them. They believe that no matter what it is that they do, they will be successful at it. They have what is known as a god complex. Everyone knows that no matter how powerful, how successful, or how superior a person is, none of us can avoid death. Because of this, the narcissist will suffer a lot of distress whenever they think about death. This is the one thing in their life that they have no power over. They are not able to control it, and they know that it could happen at any time. Death is their biggest threat.

Most importantly, the narcissist is afraid of their victims becoming strong. They are afraid that they are going to lose their power over you. They know that there is a chance that you will empower yourself with knowledge, learn about their techniques, and start seeing through the façade that they have created. They know that if you do this, you are going to quickly begin to realize that you do not have to allow them to control you any longer. They will no longer be able to get from you what they want, which was why they had you in their life in the first place. When you stop responding to their behavior and start living the life that you want to live, they panic. When you take control away from them, you show them that they no longer matter, they are unimportant, and there is nothing special about them. Sure, they can replace you easily enough and find another victim to feed off of, but knowing that they were not important to you, knowing that you were able to walk away from them no matter how much they tried to manipulate you will eat at them for the rest of their lives.

Chapter Eleven: Can a Narcissist Change?

Being in a relationship with a narcissist - whether it be at work, in a family, or in a romantic relationship - can be confusing. The relationship can become manipulative as well as abusive. Not every relationship with every narcissist will turn abusive. However, it is good to be aware that this could happen. It is also important to understand that narcissism is not a disorder. Narcissism is a trait that people have. Narcissistic Personality Disorder or NPD is a disorder that must be treated by a professional. A person can display narcissistic traits without having NPD.

Many people believe that it is impossible for anyone who displays narcissistic traits to change. The truth is that a person who is displaying narcissistic traits can change. While this change is not easy, it is possible. Once the narcissist starts focusing on the change, addressing the insecurities and loneliness that they have tried so hard to hide, they can even start to feel empathy.

Feeling empathy can be very difficult for a recovering narcissist to do. However, it is possible. To feel empathy, they are going to have to give up their need to feel superior to other people. For a narcissist to change, certain things have to occur.

First, there has to be some type of consequence to the narcissist that is meaningful to them. For example, they may lose their job or the people that they love if they do not change. One huge motivator for a narcissist to change is damage to their reputation. They may also be motivated to change if they feel that they are missing out on opportunities in their life.

They may also be motivated by the positive effects that the change will bring into their lives. For example, they will not have as many fallouts in their personal or work relationships. The relationships will begin to improve and normalize.

Therapy is something that the narcissist will need. The emotions that they have tried to hide for so long must be addressed. This is why they need to see a good therapist. You may have a strong desire to help the narcissist change, but a therapist has the training to help them do so. The therapist is going to be able to hold the narcissist accountable for their actions while not being vulnerable to their rage. If you are in a relationship with a narcissist, you will want to seek therapy as well. The two of you may also choose to take part in therapy that focuses on the relationship, apart from your personal therapy.

It is worth mentioning that some narcissists are not going to see the need to change. There are times when it does not matter what the narcissist is at risk of losing; they will not admit that they have faults or have done anything wrong. If they refuse to admit to any wrongdoings, while they need help, the chances are that they are not going to seek it out.

The following steps are going to help the narcissist change their behavior:

1. Become aware of other people's boundaries and start being considerate of them.

The narcissist tends to be unaware of where they end, and another person begins. Therefore, for them to start seeing other people as humans instead of possessions, they will want to start becoming aware of the boundaries that are set by other people. They can do this by starting to address other people by their names when they are speaking to them and when they are writing.

The narcissist is known to demand attention all of the time, which means that when they are around other people go unheard. The narcissist should focus on listening to what other people are saying. While other people are talking, they should show interest in what is being said. The narcissist misses out on a lot of opportunities to learn about life because they never listen to other people's personal experiences.

When the narcissist wants someone to do something for them, they will need to start making requests instead of making demands. They have to give the other person the space that they need to make their own choices instead of meeting the demands of the narcissist. Once they make their choice, the narcissist must respect it and not try to force the person to do what was requested of them.

2. Develop and Deliver

The narcissist is used to cheating, lying, manipulating, exaggerating, taking short cuts, not keeping commitments, and breaking promises. For them to create genuine relationships, they will have to start building trust with the people around them.

This means that they have to do what they say they are going to do. They will have to learn how to keep their promises, follow through on commitments, and keep their agreements and appointments. The best way to do this is to make sure that they are not making promises that they are not going to be able to keep. One huge mistake that narcissists and non-narcissists make is making promises or commitments that they know they are not going to be able to keep.

When the narcissist is not able to follow through with their commitments, they need to be held accountable for their actions. They also need to take the time to identify what they can do to ensure that this does not happen again. It is also very important for them to figure out what they can do to make things right with the person that they broke the promise to. This will help them learn that they are accountable for their actions.

3. Become More Mindful

Mindfulness allows one to focus on what is going on right now. For example, if you are doing eighty down the interstate, and it suddenly starts to snow, being mindful of the situation can help you quickly become aware that you need to slow down. If you were not mindful of the situation, but were instead focusing on your plans for tomorrow, you might find yourself sliding off the side of the road before you realize what is going on.

How does this help the narcissist? They can ask themselves questions like, "How is this going to be perceived by the person I am speaking to?" Or, "Am I trying to make myself look or feel superior to those around me?" Being mindful will allow the narcissist to become more aware of their actions, which in turn will help them change the behavior before someone gets hurt.

4. Ask for Help

Earlier in this book, you learned that it is very difficult for a narcissist to ask for help. They do not want to be seen as someone that depends on other people. However, by asking for help or support as they make these changes in their lives, they are going to increase their self-confidence and feel like they really belong. Instead of the illusion that people like them, they will start to see what it is like to have people care about them. Narcissists are usually very lonely because they do not let anyone get too close to them. We already talked about how they are afraid that by letting someone get too close, they will be exposed for what they really are.

If the narcissist is seriously trying to change, they should open up to at least one person in their lives. As time goes on, they will be able to open up to more and more people. Support groups are a good option for the narcissist who is afraid to open up to people and can be a small step in the right direction.

5. Forgive Themselves

As the narcissist starts to make changes in their life, they may begin to feel remorse for the pain that they have inflicted upon other people. This is completely natural; however, the narcissist may begin to think of themselves as a bad person. They will begin feeling guilt that they never felt before. This can cause them to wallow in guilt and even become depressed. It is extremely important at this point that the narcissist forgives themselves for the things that happened in the past. They may need to be reminded that the past has no bearing on what happens today. The past cannot be changed, but their future can. Do not continually bring the past up, throwing it in the narcissist's face, trying to make them feel bad about what they did. If they reach this point of change, they already feel bad enough. Instead, show them forgiveness so that they can forgive themselves.

As the narcissist works to make these changes in their life, they will return to humanity. They will be more authentic, and they are going to have much healthier relationships. They will see themselves accomplishing things that they never thought possible, and their self-confidence will be real. Soon they will begin to understand that they can make themselves feel good about who they are, and they don't have to use other people to feel that way.

Change does not happen overnight. It can take a very long time for a narcissist to be able to put all of the narcissistic traits behind them. However, as long as they continue to work toward their goal and be honest with themselves, change is possible.

Once the change has happened, it is not time to stop. Continually learning and working to improve oneself will help the narcissist create the life that they truly want. This will help them to experience true happiness and become real again.

The narcissist may have experiences for the first time that make them uncomfortable. They may experience what it is like to be hurt by another person, to be vulnerable, and to admit that they have flaws. This can be very difficult to deal with at first, and you should be prepared for some struggle. There may be times when the narcissist just wants to give up. It is so much easier for them to continue to manipulate people to get what they want in life than it is for them to work toward improving themselves and creating that life on their own.

Continue to provide support for the narcissist as long as they continue to work toward making these changes. If they are having a particularly hard time dealing with the emotions that they are going to face, remind them why they decided to make the change in the first place.

It can be hard for you as the narcissist makes these changes as well. You have already spent so much of your time trying to heal the people you harmed and trying to do whatever you could to make them happy. You may feel completely drained and as if you have nothing else to give to them, which is why you need to seek help for yourself.

Chapter Twelve: Exposing Emotional Abuse

While not everyone that has narcissistic traits has Narcissistic Personality Disorder, they can develop it. Today we hear people throwing the word narcissistic around all of the time. You may have seen it all over social media. If you have tried to do any research on emotional abuse, you may have found an overwhelming number of websites talking about narcissism. While it may feel good to give your abuser a title, it is important to make sure that this is what they are actually suffering from. Only a professional can diagnose NPD.

Some of the people who are abusive towards their partners are narcissistic, but some of them are not. Some of them are dealing with other mental disorders; some of them do not have any mental disorders whatsoever. The fact is that nothing has shown that there is a link between mental disorders and abuse.

Even if you have no idea why the person that you are with is emotionally abusing you, you need to expose the abuse. One problem that many people come across when they connect the abuse with a mental disorder is that they feel as if there is nothing that can be done about it. They accept the abuse because that is just how the person is.

It makes them feel that they have no control over the situation and that they must deal with it.

Some people may start to believe that if they could only get a diagnosis for their partner, the abuse would stop. If only the partner took medication for the disorder, they would not have to suffer the abuse any longer. Sadly, medication is not the answer. Medication can treat mental disorders, but it is not going to change abusive behavior. The abuse would have to be addressed separately from the mental disorder.

Abusing someone is a choice that is made by the abuser. People who are suffering from mental disorders are not always in control of the choices that they make, so that sort of abuse could improve with the treatment of a mental disorder, though this is rarely the case.

An abusive partner can control their behaviors such as choosing to push limits to see how much they can get away with. For example, it may start as verbal abuse, but then they slap their partner to see if they can get away with it. The person is in control of the way that they behave if they are only abusive towards you. Do they have the ability to treat other people with respect? If this is the case, they are choosing to be abusive.

They may also choose to intensify the abuse as time goes on. A person who has a mental disorder will generally behave the same way most of the time. However, an abusive person's behavior will escalate as the relationship progresses.

You need to understand that whether your partner has a mental disorder or not, they do not have the right to abuse you in any way. You are never going to be able to fix them or get them to change their behavior. It is your responsibility to stand up for yourself and start taking action.

Abuse can take on many different forms. One of those forms is emotional abuse. Because there are no physical signs of emotional abuse, it can be hard to detect. When many people think of emotional abuse, they tend to believe that it is not as serious as physical abuse. However, it is just as dangerous and can cause a lot of damage to the victim.

Emotional abuse can lead to the victim suffering from PTSD, depression, anxiety, low self-esteem, and a low sense of self-worth.

Before we go into how you can get help, let's go over a few *myths* that people tend to believe about emotional abuse.

1. Many people believe that *emotional abuse and physical abuse always happen together.* The truth is that a person can be a victim of emotional abuse without ever being a victim of physical abuse. This is what makes it so hard for those outside of the relationship to spot.

2. *Women are the victims of emotional abuse.* Emotional abuse is like any other type of abuse, and men, as well as women, can fall victim to it. Emotional abuse usually happens within a romantic relationship, but it can also occur in families or between friends.

3. *Emotional abuse isn't as bad as physical abuse.* All abuse is hurtful. Comparing one type of abuse to another type of abuse is absurd. No one has the right to judge the amount of pain that a victim has experienced and claim that another form of abuse is worse. Abuse is abuse. No matter what type of abuse you are experiencing, you deserve to be free from it.

Sign of Emotional Abuse

Do you think that you could be the victim of emotional abuse? If you suspect that you are emotionally abused, it is time for you to reach out for help. Asking for help is one of the bravest things that you will ever do. There is help out there for you.

There are many different ways for you to reach out for help:

• Go to someone that you trust and tell them what is going on. If you go to church, this could be your pastor. You can go to a trusted friend or another family member. If you are a minor, find an adult you trust, for instance, a teacher or the principal at your school, and talk to them about what is going on. Tell whoever you go to that you need to speak to them privately, which is going to allow them to really hear what you are saying, and it will provide you with a safe environment. It can be very hard to talk to another person about the abuse that you have been experiencing. Tell them as much as you can without making yourself uncomfortable. Take things as slowly as you need to, but make sure that you are sticking to the facts. Don't worry if you become emotional and break down, they are going to understand, and it is going to provide you with some emotional relief.

- If you are a child who is suffering abuse, call child protective services, or seek out the social worker at your school. You can look online to find the phone number for child-protection services in your state. You do not even have to give them your name when you call. Just tell them what is going on, and they will investigate. A worker, as well as a police officer, will be sent to your home, and they will talk to you privately about the situation.

- Contact the police. If you are in physical danger, call 911 immediately. Do not wait and ask for help later. Do not allow anyone to hurt you. If you are not in immediate danger, you can call the non-emergency number to talk to an officer about a pattern of abuse. If you are the victim, the dispatcher will ask you if you are safe or if you feel safe. After you have talked to the dispatcher, an officer will be dispatched to your location. If you do not want the officer to come to your home, you should go to the police station to give the report. Make sure that you tell the police everything but stick to the facts. You will want to bring any evidence with you to give to the police. Give the police as much information as possible, but if you are unclear about something that they have asked you, don't be afraid to let them know. Finally, make sure that you are available if the police officer needs to follow up. You should never call and ask for updates on the investigation. The police are not going to be able to give you that type of information. If the abuser does end up getting arrested, the prosecutor may contact you asking that you testify against the accused. If you are afraid to do this, you do not have to; no one is going to make you testify.

• Sometimes reaching out to the police can seem overwhelming. If you need to talk to someone, express what you are feeling or if you are unsure that what you are going through is abuse, you can text HELLO to 741741. This will connect you to a crisis counselor. If the abuser has access to your phone, make sure that you delete the messages after the conversation has ended.

• Create a safety plan. Even if you are not suffering from physical abuse, you need to make sure that you have a safety plan. Think of places that you can go to get away from the abuser. Create a plan that you can follow when you are ready to get out of the relationship. Make sure that you know where you will go, who you will contact, and how you will survive. Be as detailed as possible so that when the time comes, you do not have to worry about anything.

Dealing with Emotional Abuse

If you are in an emotionally abusive relationship, remember that you deserve to be treated with respect and love. No one deserves to suffer from abuse. It can take time for you to recover from the abuse that you have suffered. You need to put yourself first and practice self-care.

You can start your recovery by talking to a professional. You are going to need help processing everything that has happened to you and the emotions that come with the abuse. Some therapists have been trained to work specifically with abuse survivors. The therapist is going to be able to teach you how to cope with the abuse and all of your emotions.

Learning how to practice self-care is very important if you have been in any type of abusive relationship. You have been taking care of your abuser for so long that you likely have not been taking care of yourself. Start focusing on you for once, which will help reduce any anxiety or depression that you are dealing with due to the abuse. Focus on providing your body with the healthy food that it needs, getting enough exercise, reading a book, spending time doing the things that you enjoy the most. Make yourself and your health a priority.

Start building strong and healthy friendships. Don't try to jump into a new relationship while you are healing from an abusive one. Instead, focus on making new friends and finding the right people. Start taking a class, learn something new, or spend some time working on something that you enjoy with a group of people.

Emotional abuse can be very damaging, but there are things that you can do to protect yourself and to take control of your life back. You should never feel that you are stuck in a situation because you are being abused. You can find your way out, and you can live a happy and fulfilling life.

Conclusion: Thriving after a Narcissistic Relationship

Once you have broken free from a narcissistic relationship, you may find it hard to move on. This is not uncommon when a person has been in a relationship with a narcissist.

The narcissist expected special treatment from you whether they did things to deserve this treatment or not. They only way that the narcissist can satisfy their fragile ego is by putting others down. They love to make you feel as if you cannot live without them. I have good news for you. You are not only going to be able to survive without them, but you are going to be able to thrive.

One of the best pieces of knowledge that you can have as you move forward with your life is that the narcissist that you were in a relationship with could not think of anyone else but themselves. They are only focused on what makes them feel good. Chances are you want to make sure that you never end up in another relationship with a narcissist again. How can you do this? By thriving.

Look at it like this; if you had high self-esteem when you met the narcissist, the chances are that they would not have been interested in you. The narcissist wants to be in a relationship with someone that they can control, someone that is going to make them feel superior. If a person has a healthy level of self-confidence, they may make the mistake of getting into a relationship with a narcissist, but the relationship will be cut short. They will recognize that there is a problem within the relationship and move on with their life. More importantly than that, they refuse to accept the blame for the relationship not working out. Instead, they understand that the relationship was not working, and they are focused on their own happiness. They are not willing to accept any relationship that adds no value to their lives.

To make sure that you do not end up in another relationship like this again, you will want to start focusing on you. Start by believing in yourself. Focus on creating the life that you want and becoming the person that you want to be. Focus on your career, your dreams, and your hopes. Take the time to finally focus on your health or learning that new skill you have always wanted to learn. Spend time doing the things that you love and building your self-esteem.

Perhaps at some point early on in the relationship, you started to wonder how such an amazing person might have wanted to be with you. That should have been your first clue that something was wrong. When you focus on building your self-confidence, you will never question why someone would want to be with you. If you are working on overcoming your relationship with a narcissist, you need to remember that you are amazing.

Narcissists are very picky about who they date. They want to be with someone successful and accomplished. They also want to be with someone who downplays who they really are. *Now* is the time for you to rise to the top. It is time for you to embrace who you are and move on with your life.

Ask yourself what was it that made the narcissist feel that they could target you. Are you neglecting yourself in an area of your life that makes you an easy target for the narcissist? Are you putting yourself down? Do you feel that other people are better than you are? Do you put other people down so that you can feel better about yourself? Some of the narcissist's traits may be mirrored in you. What you should focus on, however, is what trait is causing the biggest issue for you. How are you allowing that trait to affect your life? Learning from this experience is the best way to make sure that you do not repeat this mistake in the future.

This can be a lot for a person to absorb. Remember, we are not trying to focus on making you feel poorly about yourself. Instead, it is about ensuring that you can thrive in your life while ensuring that you never fall victim to a narcissist again.

You have suffered both mentally and emotionally. This can cause many people to completely collapse and become a victim for the rest of their lives. Some people also turn into abusers themselves because they begin to take on the tendencies of the narcissist. I want better for you.

You don't have to be a victim any longer. Once you have ended the relationship, you can accept that to be true. It is time for you to move forward in your life without abuse.

To do this, you have to stop living in denial. Stop making excuses for the abuse that you suffered. It is easy to try to make excuses for the abuser. You want to feel sorry for them. You want to come up with a reason that they did the things that they did. However, if you want to move forward with your life, you simply have to accept that the abuse happened. Stop dwelling on the details. By dwelling on the details, you are allowing the abuser to continue to affect your life.

Set up boundaries that you will stick to when you enter any new relationships. Make sure that those boundaries are clear and that there are clear consequences to those boundaries being crossed. Knowing what your boundaries are will help you to protect yourself in the future.

Confront the abuse. Do not try to pretend that it did not happen. Do not allow the abuser to convince you that you should stay friends after the end of the relationship. Narcissists will do this to keep you around so that they can take advantage of you later. Confront them. Tell them what they did to you and that their behavior was not acceptable.

When you do confront them, stick to your points, and end the conversation. Narcissists are bullies. They are good at bullying. They can turn the conversation around and place the blame on you, which is one of the ways they are able to keep their victims around for so long.

Cut the narcissist off. Do not have any contact with them after the relationship has ended. If they want to meet up and talk, tell them no. This can be very difficult, but it is the best thing for you.

Finally, you need to move on with your life. Choose to focus on the life that you want and create that life. When you are busy creating the life that you want, you are not going to have time to focus on the abuser or the abuse.

Many people think that it is impossible to move on after they have been in an abusive relationship. They tell themselves that they are always going to be the victim and that they did something to deserve the pain that they endured. You did not do anything to deserve the abuse, and you no longer have to be the victim.

So, start right now. Start focusing on that life that you deserve. Start working on becoming a person whom a narcissist will never target because they know they would not get away with abusing them.

Part 2: Gaslighting

What You Need to Know About this Type of Manipulation and How Narcissists Can Use It Against You in an Abusive Relationship

What You Need to Know About
this Type of Manipulation and
How Narcissists Can Use It Against You
in an Abusive Relationship

TYRON BRADEN

Introduction

Gaslighting - What You Need to know about this Type of Manipulation and How Narcissists Can Use It Against You in an Abusive Relationship is no ordinary book. Every now and then, some author somewhere has put out a new book with their own take on the subject. Sadly, a lot of these books do not tell you everything you need to know. At the end of each of these books, you realize it was really no different than the last. Even worse, you realize that you have no idea what to do with the information you've gleaned from that book - since there was zero guidance on how to make it all practical!

In this book, I'm going to teach you everything you need to know about gaslighting. You may feel like you've already learned all you need to about this devious manipulation technique, but this is not like any other book out there that you may have read.

Unfortunately, when you read the countless books available on the market about gaslighting and how narcissists use this technique to abuse and destroy you in a relationship, there is not quite enough information on the specific techniques. You might just read a chapter at best or a blurb at worst. Quite frankly, the information on gaslighting as a narcissistic, manipulative technique is very inadequate in many books and may even be absent. There is so much more to learn about this!

You've made a very smart decision choosing to get a copy of this book. I believe you will find it to be up to date, very informative, and very practical. It's just no good pointing out the different ways you can be gaslit by a narcissist without giving any practical examples of gaslighting in action, and practical methods to deal with the problem. Gaslighting is a very terrible technique indeed, with far-reaching implications if one cannot recognize it for what it is or take action to protect themselves. To really tackle gaslighting and narcissists, one needs to do a lot better than simply spotting well-known facts.

Is there a narcissist or two in your life making every day miserable for you? How would you like to put the kibosh on their gaslighting tactics, and reclaim control of your life once and for all? You deserve to live your best life. This implies, among other things, that you do not allow toxic situations or people to steal your joy and peace. Toxic people are real, as are the problems they create. The answer isn't always to avoid them, or to bend over for them every time until they suck the very life out of you. It's all about knowing exactly how to skillfully handle them in such a way that they get the message: You're not a victim. You will no longer allow yourself to be trifled with.

Most books just dump facts on you. This book is different. By the end of this book, you will know how to deal with gaslighting so that you always have your dignity and sanity intact.

Chapter One: What Manipulation Is - And What It Feels Like

How can you tell when you're being manipulated? How can you tell when someone is messing with your mind and your emotions, hoping to exploit you for their own selfish, nasty benefit?

Sometimes you can almost swear that this person you're dealing with is up to no good. You have a nagging feeling in the back of your mind that something is not quite right here. It feels like nothing is as it seems every time you speak to this person. You want to give them the benefit of the doubt, but you just can't. You start to wonder if you're not really the crazy one here. After all, look at all the paranoid thoughts you have swimming around in your mind like a not-so-adorable school of fish!

When you're being manipulated psychologically, you feel as though your thoughts are being deliberately influenced toward the wrong conclusions and decisions. It feels as if your emotions are being taken advantage of, even if you're unable to put your finger on how and why it's working. You feel like you're losing control. You're not coming from a place of power in a manipulative interaction.

Aren't We Always Being Manipulated?

Now, it's easy to answer yes to this question. It would seem like there is a pretty thin line between innocent social influence and malevolent manipulation. The line is not really that thin. It's not unusual for people to socially influence one another. It's all a part of relating to one another in a healthy way. So how can you tell the difference between this healthy interaction and manipulation? Well, when you're being manipulated, it feels as if this person doing the manipulating is using you for their own benefit, at your own expense. They have an agenda, and you can feel it as they bend and twist you around to get what they want. The trouble is that they're so slick at it, you begin to doubt your gut feelings about what's going on — and that is just one of the goals of the manipulator.

How to Find Out if You're A Victim of Manipulation

Now, we're going to run through a list of questions you should ask yourself in order to figure out whether you're the victim of emotional and psychological manipulation. Call to mind the relationships or friendships which constantly leave you wondering about the other person's intentions, as you ask yourself these questions.

I want to make it clear that these questions are not necessarily the be-all and end-all when it comes to figuring out if you're a victim. However, they will let you see where, in your life. you're overtly or covertly manipulated. Please keep in mind that just because you recognize some things listed here, that does not automatically mean you're being manipulated. Sometimes, it's an innocent case where the person you're dealing with has a few unacceptable traits, and nothing more. It is important for you to recognize when you're being exploited and drained by the manipulative narcissist in your life.

Questions

1. **Do you feel like you're never on equal footing with this person?** You may have noticed that each time you interact with them, you feel like a fish out of water. It's almost like wherever the talk is happening, you're in their space, and not yours; not somewhere neutral where you feel like you have equal footing. You may have noticed that all your interactions take place, not just where they want it to, but *when they want it to.* There's never any thought given to what may be convenient for you. It feels as though you're always in their home, or their office, or their <u>insert-random-place-here</u>. You never feel like you're in a familiar, comfortable space physically or mentally when you interact with them.

2. **Have you noticed that when you interact, you always must speak first?** You may have noticed that when you meet, you're the first one to open your mouth. Inevitably, you feel vulnerable. You feel as if since you've had to speak first, you're basically being probed for weaknesses that can be exploited. You feel like they're working out what makes you tick so that they can hit you where it hurts. This is a great technique for making sales, but it has devastating effects when your narcissistic partner uses it against you.

3. **When you interact with them, do you feel that they always find a way to bend or twist the facts?** They tell a lie, and you feel confused because you're not sure why they felt the need to lie. They make excuses, and while you feel like those are some terrible excuses, you don't want to be an inconsiderate bully by making them accountable for their actions. You want to make things work, but they choose to blame you — even if an objective third party, the United Nations, and everyone's grandma would attest to the fact that it was their fault, not yours. They say something that sounds like the truth, but history and your gut make you feel like it's not the truth. It's just their version of events. You've noticed that they only ever tell you things when they feel it will serve them, and they have a habit of keeping important

information from you. You've noticed every time they open their mouth, they're either understating the facts so that you feel like you're just an overly dramatic nut-job making Mount Rushmore out of a pebble. When they're not understating things, they're exaggerating them, so that you feel like the lovechild of Frankenstein and the Loch Ness Monster!

4. **Does this person weigh you down with their intellect and intelligence?** You may have noticed that you always feel like a fool when you speak with them. They'll bully you intellectually as they dump all the stats and facts on you so that they can take advantage of you - *since you only know so much.* You feel like since they have all the facts, you have no choice but to go along with whatever agenda they are pushing. Sometimes it's for a specific goal. Other times, they just love to lord it over you.

5. **When you talk, do they have a habit of always expressing negative emotions and yelling?** Some manipulators use their voices to bully others so that they can get what they want. If you always tend to feel small, insignificant, and shut down because they're yelling at you, chances are it's no accident. Not only do they get louder and louder, they may become very theatrical with their bodies, as well. You feel like the only way to end that is to give in. They also have no issues doing this with others around, so that you feel embarrassed and ashamed. Others won't yell. They'll just be so obvious about their disappointment or pain that you won't submit to their will, that you begin to feel bad about standing up for yourself. This is a more subtle form of manipulation, with the end goal of forcing you to give them what they want.

6. **Do you find yourself constantly surprised (in a bad way) and out of balance when you're with this person?** Surprises can be nice. They can also be nasty. You may have noticed that this person is a huge fan of the nasty kind of surprises. They spring a "surprise" on you, and you feel off-balance immediately, as your mind struggles to make

sense of things, and your emotions do exactly what the manipulator wants. You get these surprises, and you feel like you can't do anything to counter them. You can't make any plans to be able to deal with them.

7. **Does this person always issue you ultimatums?** You feel a lot of pressure to say or do something you otherwise wouldn't, because they've given you a directive: either do *this*, or you will have to do *that*. You know deep down that there are other options, but with them, it's either A or B. There are no other letters of the alphabet that they know! You feel the pressure to act, and you do, giving in to whatever they wanted from you.

8. **Do they make a habit of making jokes at your expense?** You may have noticed that this manipulative person loves to make wisecracks about you. They do this when there are others around you, making you feel incompetent or stupid. At times, they do it when it's just the two of you, to make you feel like you're making something into a big deal; never mind that it really is a big deal. Whatever the case may be, the jokes they make are designed to make you feel inferior. You feel insecure. You feel cut down, even if they're grinning. That's the plan. The end game is to be the top dog, psychologically speaking.

9. **Do they criticize and judge you to no end?** A true manipulator will do this, and not bother to offer you constructive feedback, or suggestions for how you can get better at whatever they're criticizing you for. You get the sense that they couldn't care less about helping you to become better. If they do, you will notice that you always feel "less than" around them. You feel like you're never good enough. They nitpick, and judge, and criticize, and they do it with a light tone of voice and a smile. Maybe they even throw in a warm, loving touch for good measure. However, you find yourself constantly feeling like you're being ridiculed. You feel your ideas and thoughts are being dismissed. You're marginalized into nothingness. You feel like you

give a 110%, and no matter how hard you try or how much better you get, you're always going to be less than valuable in their eyes.

10. **Do they give you the silent treatment until you do or say what they want?** They stonewall you, and you feel powerless to do anything about the situation at hand. All attempts at communication on your part are ignored, making you feel even more helpless. The manipulator knows this. You feel like you're stuck waiting, and for what? You have no idea. The longer they make you wait, the more you feel uneasy, uncertain, and doubtful of your stance. They'll hold out if they need to, staying silent unless and until they feel like they have punished you enough, or until you cave in and give them what they want.

11. **Have you noticed that this person is in the habit of playing dumb?** They like to feign ignorance about what your wants and needs are — never mind that you've told them in 500, 2,500, 6.000 different ways and times! You feel exasperated by this, and you don't know what else to do, other than to put up and shut up.

12. **Do most interactions with this person involve you being guilt-tripped?** There are so many ways this can happen. The manipulator is great at shifting blame in such a way that if you're not careful, you really will take it on. You start to feel terrible for stuff that has nothing to do with you. Your weaknesses and soft spots are shamelessly exploited by the manipulator so that you have no choice but to do as they ask.

13. **Does this person have a knack of playing the victim even when they clearly aren't?** You may have noticed they just love to be the wounded puppy. This is a great cover-up for their nasty behavior. If they have health problems, rest assured they will play them up. If they don't have health problems, they will make them up. You feel like every word out of their mouth, every action they take is carefully crafted to pull you in, make you feel sorry for them, or make you want to do something for them. You may have noticed that in every story, they are either the weak and defenseless one, or they are the self-

sacrificing savior. This is all to make you do something out of the goodness of your heart or to exploit your moral sense of duty.

If you answered yes to most of these questions, then it's obvious who and what you're dealing with here. A manipulator. A thought-bender, filling your mind with whatever he/she likes. An emotion-bender, making you feel whatever will work for them in the end.

If you suspect that you might be in a relationship with a narcissist, don't just sit around and do nothing! Please seek professional help immediately, with a licensed psychiatrist or a professional in the mental health sector, so you can get advice that suits you and your unique situation.

Chapter Two: Types and Traits of Narcissism

You're probably reading this book because you have the misfortune of dealing with a narcissist in your life. Maybe this narcissist is your romantic partner. However, how can you be certain this person is really a narcissist, and you're not just upset because of this one mistake they made? Before we begin talking about the different kinds of narcissists that exist, perhaps it would be best for us to first define a narcissist.

Meet the Narcissist

The word "narcissist" is often thrown around when discussing politicians, celebrities, or that one friend of yours who just loves looking good and needs to check themselves out in every remotely reflective surface that they pass. However, not everyone knows what narcissism means.

In today's social media-obsessed world, where people will do anything for clout, narcissism reigns supreme. How many followers do you have? What is your brand? Wait for a second, before you answer that, let me take a selfie. This is the world we live in today; there are tons of YouTubers who go on for a quarter of an hour, maybe more, talking about their results with a mewing, or their latest experiment with an all-new makeup line. You've got the Kanyes, who pronounce themselves as a god; the Bernie Madoff and Elizabeth Holmes, ripping people off for billions of dollars without any shame or remorse, getting people to buy into their grandiose, false ideas.

Narcissists are everywhere. Lots of actors, musicians, politicians, businessmen, presidents, producers, athletes, directors, and other famous people are narcissists — so many of them that it is easy to assume that narcissists are only those who have power and influence or are leaders in one field or another. However, this is not the case. The narcissist can be the lovely colleague who is always so helpful, your high-achieving boss, the cheerful neighbor, or the angelic-looking face fast asleep next to you as you read this right now.

According to the fifth edition of the Diagnostic and Statistical Manual of Mental Disorders, narcissistic personality disorder presents as a constant pattern of grandiose expressions, the need to be admired, and a very curious absence of empathy. It's not that they can't be empathetic; it's that they don't know how to empathize. This disorder has other markers such as a very sensitive, fragile sense of self-worth, as well as obvious or hidden expressions of grandiosity.

Your typical narcissist is all about the superficial things, like the perfect kind of love, outrageous success, or unearthly beauty. These are the sorts of things they value over stuff like meaningful relationships with others, or emotions. If life were a pool, you'd find your narcissist in the kiddie area, because they just cannot handle any depth. They believe that they are unique. They're special, unlike the rest of us normal people. They're some of the most entitled people you will ever meet. They do a sport of exploiting others around them. They are complete strangers to empathy, and if they do have any relationships at all, you can bet that they're all very superficial. Empathy is an underused, atrophied muscle for the narcissist.

Pathologically speaking, narcissism is a disorder that severely affects the sufferer's self-esteem. I know that seems implausible given the way we've just defined the narcissist but stick with me here. If you strip away that larger-than-life facade, take away that seemingly never-ending quest to be the greatest, and get a peek behind all that grandiosity, you won't find more of these things. What you will notice is that all that shine is nothing but tinsel. They have no control over their feelings and only live for the love and admiration of others. If they get it, then life's good! If they don't, then life is ruined for them.

Types of Narcissists

Most people assume that narcissists are those who are constantly concerned about their appearance or something else on a superficial level. This is probably in large part due to the mythological story about Narcissus, the young man who fell in love with his reflection. However, as you've probably already figured out from everything written here, narcissism is a lot more than just an obsession with one's looks. To really get a clear picture of this disorder, let's take a quick look at the four types of narcissists that you can find.

The **grandiose narcissist** is just that: Grandiose. They talk big. They want you to think of them as the big kahuna. They're loud and brag a lot. You simply must pay attention to how awesome they are. There is no one as good as they are as far as they are concerned, and they won't let you forget that in a hurry. They're all about flash. If there is some place where they think will give them the prestige to be seen at, you can bet your bottom dollar they're going to be there! If there are people they think of as having "status," you bet they will do all they can to not only connect with them, but also make sure you know that they have a connection with them – even if it was a 15-second elevator ride with George Clooney. You're going to know about it, and they're much better than you can ever hope to be because of it. Oh, and you can bet that 15 seconds will be 15 minutes, and they got invited to Clooney's luxurious home in Malta!

The **malignant narcissist** is the worst of the lot. Not only are they everything the grandiose narcissist is, *but they are also mean.* They're okay with stealing, cheating, and lying. They would make the very best of criminals. The only slight difference between the malignant narcissist and a psychopath is that unlike the psychopath, they would probably feel a bit bad about their actions. Even then, they'd probably only feel that way if the person they hurt was one of their own, i.e., family. However, if the person they hurt is someone they don't know, then they couldn't care less about them - or about the terrible consequences of their actions.

The **covert narcissist** is the kind who often flies under the radar. You might never peg them for a narcissist, because after all, your typical narcissist is perfect in their own eyes, and would never admit to bad stuff happening to them ... *or would they?* The covert narcissist is always the martyr. They're always put upon by the world. They go on and on about their sacrifices, or how they could have achieved greatness in this, that, or the other field if it weren't for technology, their bum knee, or the world – which, for some daft reason, perpetually remains blind to their awesomeness. The covert narcissist can often come off seeming depressed. However, even with treatment for depression, the covert narcissist can only make so much improvement. They perpetually remain stuck in bad situations. They are overly sensitive to criticism. They're the ones who say stuff like, "Woe unto the world, for it, never did see my greatness!" Okay, maybe they don't say it that dramatically, but they do show a tendency towards theatrics. How else can they get the attention that every kind of narcissist wants and needs?

The **communal narcissist** is another kind of narcissist that you just might miss. These are the ones who are always saving the world in one way or another — and they have the pictures to prove it. They can't just do good things for others without having to announce it! They want to be recognized and validated for their good work. It's like they're saying, "Look at how awesome I am, helping these people out!" The funny, yet sad, thing about this is that they have zero connection to the people or pets they're trying to save or the causes that they advocate, and they're not even trying to establish one. It's all about *getting seen doing good*, having some movement or cause or hospital wing named after them, and nothing more. (At least this is one of those times narcissism does the world some good.)

Red Flags of Narcissism

There are so many classic traits that you can use to spot the narcissist in your life. For instance, they have an intense desire for the world to think of them in a certain way, and as such, are very particular about their image. They would go so far as emulating every small detail about people they consider worthy of copying. Think Elizabeth Holmes, who began dressing like Steve Jobs - and even gave presentations the same way Jobs did. She was so obsessed was she with her image that she even deliberately lowered the tone of her voice to give it more authority - or whatever else she was going for.

Another dangerous tip-off is that narcissists will lie about the weirdest things. They lie even when it's not necessary. They're so comfortable with lying that you'll never catch them by looking at out for the usual body language of a liar. To them, they're just talking. They can get away with things because most people assume there is no way anyone would be so comfortable with lying without a few obvious "tells."

That said, the narcissist's brain processes the act of lying differently than we do, so you cannot look for signs of them being disturbed as proof of their lies. You're better off considering everything they've told you from a holistic point of view, putting it all together, and checking with your gut as to whether it all rings true. They'll lie, and they'll double down on that lie even if you catch them with their pants down.

Now, let's dive into the various red flags you should watch for to tell whether the person you're dealing with is a ***textbook narcissist***.

Red Flags for Narcissists

1.   Zero Empathy. Kathy and Tom are a couple, but not the happiest couple by any stretch of the imagination. Tom was doing his best to keep things on the up and up financially, while Kathy was mostly unavailable to him. From the outside looking in, it seemed like the two were only together because it was easier than going their separate ways. She knew he was having a lot of money issues, yet she hardly ever wants to be with him because it means she will have to spend a few bucks on food. However, she is more than generous with her friends and coworkers, as well as clients she deems worth impressing. In short, she's okay with spending her money on others if it serves her purposes.   She would come to his home late, making sure she had already had a bite to eat so she wouldn't have to spend money getting him dinner; or she eats whatever he has at home.

Tom was having some trouble at work one day, and she just decided to show up after a phone call - without asking him. In her mind, she was supportive. Tom, wanting to keep the peace, did not make Kathy leave. What did Kathy do? She did nothing but go on and on about how terribly he's handling things at work, and how he could have done things a lot better. That wasn't all, though. She told him that he had messed up her day — even though he never asked her to come over! At the end of the day, they both went out for dinner. It was somewhere Kathy had picked out, and it was very pricey. She knew this, yet she told him, "You owe me dinner after the day you've put me through." So, Tom, having no choice, spent about $75 on dinner. Kathy never bothered to help. She thanked him for dinner, ever so smugly. Then she told him he's "so darned lucky" to have her in his life at all.

This is just a scenario that shows you how incredibly lacking in empathy the narcissist is! The narcissist is just not able to recognize how others feel or what they're going through. They can't identify with whatever you're struggling with. The reason is simple: You're not them. They are the only thing that matters in the whole world, so you and your issues do not exist as far as they are concerned.

The narcissist will do and say whatever they want with not even a thought for how their words and actions might affect you. A narcissist will do the cruelest things and say the meanest things because, well, because they are narcissists! They can be very unaware of how much pain they are causing you. Other times - especially with the malignant narcissist - they know exactly what they're doing.

When the narcissist is feeling upset, they expect everyone else to feel the same way. If they're ecstatic, then the whole world should be ecstatic, too. Who cares that you just lost your dog when they just bought the latest iPhone? You'd better be excited for them too; otherwise, they'll say you're jealous, you're never happy for them, or you're killing their vibes. A narcissist is an interesting person in that they never seek to understand others, yet they desire to be understood. All they ever do is take and take, but never give.

Think of the narcissist as a mirror. You look in it, but you don't see yourself. There's nothing there. You feel so confused as to how anyone can be so lacking in empathy. You wonder why you're feeling so left out, and incredibly misunderstood. It isn't you! Don't take that on yourself. It's the narcissist's inability to connect with others or identify with anyone who isn't them.

When you're in a relationship with a narcissist, you feel like you're never seen and never heard. You're never touched — at least not like you used to be in the beginning when he was love-bombing you, sucking you into his clutches. Being in a relationship with a narcissist means the only time you're ever noticed is *when you will be of use.*

The sad thing about being in a relationship that is short on empathy: it's hard to connect with each other. You spend every day and night frustrated, as you seek out ways to connect with this empty, hollow shell of a person who is causing you so much pain. There's no real communication or connection between you two, because one of you just doesn't give a damn - and won't even try.

The narcissist assumes that the things that matter to them matter to everyone else. Therefore, you'll notice they can get going on whatever they feel is the hottest thing in their life, and they won't shut up about it or let you get a word in edgewise. Even when you do say something, they find a way to hijack the conversation and make it about themselves. They'll share all their problems with you, but the second you open your mouth, they aren't so patient. They want you to wrap it up quickly - even if you just heard them out, even providing them with some great advice. They'll choose that moment to play with their hands, check their social media, and zone out.

Pay attention to how the narcissist listens, and you'll notice that they *barely do.* They'll be distracted, looking around, even yawning as you try to share what's going on with you. When you're about to get into a relationship with someone, pay attention to the way they listen to you. This is a great way to figure out whether this person has any empathy at all. If they can't shut up, listen, and really show that they understand how you are feeling, then there is no empathy, which means there's no point in starting a relationship with them.

2.   **Grandiosity.** "I am way smarter than anyone else in this class, but I do my best not to brag about it. I'm well on my way to securing an internship at the most prestigious law firm. My mother has connections with a lot of powerful people in the country, so I'm going to be just fine. By the way, I met Mr. Cartright - he's a multimillionaire and the guy who's going to be my boss — I just call him Ben now, because you know, we're on a first-name basis, and not to brag, but he's definitely in love with me. He just couldn't get enough of my ideas! So, yeah, even if I'm just going to start off as a lowly intern, nothing too fancy, you better believe I won't last in that position long. I'm going to get to the top fast. Also, since daddy and Ben play golf together, and since I'm incredibly intelligent, I know I'll make senior partner in a year, or even less. I'm going to win every single case that comes my way. I'm just that good at everything I do, you know? Of course, you know!"

You probably know someone like this. They exaggerate how great they are and how valuable they are. They want you to think that they have all the power connections and have the very best experiences. Now, none of this needs to be real. The grandiose narcissist is completely fine with making up these bogus fantasy worlds if they think it will make them look good in everyone's eyes. In reality, they really haven't done all that much in their lives. They love to go on and on about their future plans. If they meet a celeb once, you can rest assured they're going to have a thousand and one stories spun from that *one* meeting.

The grandiose narcissist believes that no one matters as much as they do. Everything about them is larger than life — at least, that's what they would have you believe. They don't want recognition alone; they want a temple for you (a sad, poor normie) to worship them in so that they can feel good about themselves.

There are some narcissists who are already accomplished in one aspect of life or another. They can still be grandiose, in that they'll just keep going on and on about all the stuff that they have accomplished, all the stuff they have, and all the unique experiences that could only ever happen to them or someone of their "status." They're loads of fun at first when you listen to them. They are interested in people who are famous, beautiful, or outrageously rich. They talk a big game, but sooner or later, you'll notice that they never really follow through on their dreams. That doesn't mean they'll shut up about it. And woe unto you if you ever mention that they're all talk and no action! They value themselves way too highly while undervaluing others.

When it comes to grandiosity in love, you'd better watch out. Narcissists are all about the perfect love story. They'll wax poetic about it, sweeping you completely off your feet in the beginning. Everything about them just feels magical and unreal! And that's because it's all unreal. They have unrealistic expectations of relationships, and as a result, they are hardly ever satisfied with whoever they end up with. If you hear the words, "the greatest love story" (or something to that effect), and you've noticed it's always being thrown about, you'd better run.

3. Entitlement. The narcissist believes they deserve special treatment. Why? Well, they don't need a reason. They believe that everyone simply must go along with their demands, regardless of whether there is any logic to them. They don't feel they should wait in line for anything.

They believe that they should get no less than the very best. Everyone else exists to serve them as far as they are concerned. There are rules, sure, but these rules never apply to them as far as they are concerned. Everything must be done exactly the way that they want it. Either that or forget about it.

It doesn't help that we live in a world where entitlement is encouraged, especially if you're dealing with someone who is powerful, wealthy, or has some other form of status. When people get used to others bending over backward to please them, it can be quite a shock on the rare occasion when someone stands up to them. Now, this is not to insinuate that every entitled person you meet is a narcissist. I'm merely saying that some people just get used to the feeling of entitlement. For the narcissist, they judge their place in the world based on the way others perceive and treat them. For this reason, they crave and feel entitled to very special treatment. The narcissist is the person you'll see insulting waiters or the bartender because they feel they're not properly attended to — never mind whether that is true or not.

When it comes to relationships, entitlement can cause a lot of heartache for the non-narcissistic partner, whose needs are often ignored, if they are even noticed at all. Other times, entitlement can show up in bouts of arrogance, as the narcissist considers others to be less than they are. Notice the way your partner interacts with others who are lower on the totem or money pole. Notice the way they interact with service providers. If they're terrible, rude, condescending, yelling, or whatever, then you could be dating a narcissist. *There is no reason good enough to be mean to others.*

4. Manipulation. The narcissist is manipulative. They can't help it, that's just the way that they are. The narcissist is a pro at bending thoughts, emotions, and situations so that they can have whatever they want. They are the ultimate spin masters. You'll find that when you deal with the narcissist in your life, you constantly feel drained and exhausted, trying to keep up with their devious schemes. The result is that you give in and give them whatever it is that they want.

The narcissist is a pro at spinning the truth in such a way that it works to their advantage. For instance, if they don't want to pull their own weight financially by getting a job, they might spin a story about how their father's treatment of them as a child devastated their sense of self-worth so much that they would never be able to hold down a job. Then there's you, with the bleeding heart, deciding you're going to take on a couple more jobs so that your poor baby doesn't have to grow up and do hard, adult stuff like working.

Narcissists are so good at manipulating that sometimes you don't realize it's going on, and you don't see it until it's too late. When it finally does hit you, you wonder why you didn't notice. You may feel stupid and blind for not seeing it. Don't beat yourself up; most of us don't stand a chance against a narcissist! We're not living every day filled with cynicism, so it's only natural not to suspect what's going on.

5.   Rage and Anger. Your classic narcissist is only a breath away from raging out. They are okay with violence, throwing stuff, yelling, door-slamming, or threatening to hit you. They're cool with just storming out of the room because they can.

Now, there's nothing wrong with anger. It's a natural emotion and not an odd response. The thing about anger is that it exists on a spectrum. On one end, you've got anger that you keep in check so that your responses are reasonable and possibly productive. On the other end of that spectrum: pure, unfiltered rage, beyond control - and this is where the narcissist is very comfortable. For the narcissist, rage allows them to control the reactions of others around them so that they get their way. These are the people you need to "walk on eggshells" around because there's no telling when they'll explode.

One of the telltale signs you're dealing with a raging narcissist is to observe the way that they drive. Do they make a habit of driving erratically, cutting others off, tailgating them? If so, you may be dealing with a narcissist. One of the things about the narcissist and their rage is that they can never really hide it. One way or another, it will manifest. If you insist on continuing the relationship with this person, you will find that the raging bull is going to make you its waving red flag. And, it will charge at you, *full speed.*

6. **Paranoia.** In this case, I'm not talking about the kind of paranoia you'd get like with flat-earthers. I'm talking about the fact the narcissist constantly feels like everyone is out to get them. Everyone hates them or is jealous of them. The trouble with this constant paranoia is that they enter a relationship with you on the defensive — which means you often feel attacked when you're with them. You get the sense that you're never fully trusted, and you're fighting some battle that you don't understand. Not only do you feel confused by the narcissist's paranoia, but you also feel worn out by it.

In your relationship with the narcissist, they often make you feel like you just can't be trusted. You feel like you need to guard the way you interact with others because it's very easy for the narcissist to see something innocent and immediately assume you slept with their buddy Josh, his wife, and all of Josh's buddies as well. The narcissist will accuse you of not being supportive enough of their dreams, or of planning to betray them. The funny thing is the narcissist will punish you with their paranoia for the very same things that they do and get away with. Did you raise your hand to get the waiter's attention? Well, you're obviously a flirt, and you sleep around. However, when they stare at the waiter's cute butt with no regard for the fact that you're right there and can see them checking someone else out, then you're just deliberately turning a non-issue into something to argue about.

One huge sign that your narcissistic partner is paranoid is the way that they obsessively protect their cell phone. Every single app has a code for it. Their phone is locked the second they put it down. Yet, they'll constantly bug you about where you're going, who with, how long you'll be gone, and why your phone needs passwords. No one should have to be in a relationship where there is zero trust, with an overly generous helping of suspicion and paranoia.

Other Narcissistic Traits

Narcissists have a lot of things in common. They are critical, oblivious, and insensitive to other people's emotions, and lack the ability to think reflectively. You will find that no matter what you say to call them out, the narcissist will always have one excuse or another. They refuse to be held accountable! Also, everything must go the way they want it to. They're so rigid in thought that they are unwilling to consider alternatives.

You'll never find anyone who is as hypersensitive to the little things as the narcissist is. They are incapable of being happy for anyone who is not themselves. They're jealous of your success, and you can feel it put a damper on your spirits.

The narcissist does not feel the guilt that you and I feel. They have no sense of remorse, and they have no insight at all. They have a constant habit of projection, shifting blame, and guilt (that they rightly deserve) over to you, so that you start to buy into their spiel.

The narcissist is a liar, always putting on a show because they need to be constantly praised, admired, or validated. We've all got varying degrees of vanity going on, but with the narcissist, this vanity is to the tenth degree.

The narcissist is a distant and cold person. When they do engage, you'll find them very controlling and unpredictable. Whatever emotion you get is probably going to be a case of schadenfreude (pleasure derived from another person's misfortune) forever at your expense. Far be it from the narcissist to commiserate with you — unless it serves them in one way or another to do so. They're selfish, incredibly greedy, and have no sense of boundaries when it comes to how they treat others.

Chapter Three: Gaslighting - The Narcissist's Favorite Tool of Manipulation

The narcissist is a manipulator at heart. Of all the tools the narcissist loves to use to bend you to their will, their favorite tool is gaslighting. Gaslighting is a devious manipulation technique in which the narcissist has you wondering whether you're losing your mind. The narcissist plants doubt and uncertainty in your mind for the sole purpose of gaining control over you.

You know yourself. You know your thoughts, opinions, and beliefs. You know exactly what you stand for, and what you don't — or at least you used to. However, since the narcissist came into your life, you've found yourself feeling very unsure and confused about everything. You're not sure you remember things right anymore. You're never certain about your decisions. You find yourself constantly paranoid, wondering if you can trust your own mind. You start to think you're going nuts, when in fact you aren't. It's just that the narcissist has successfully gaslit you.

The Origin of "Gaslighting"

The term "gaslighting" became accepted lingo thanks to the 1944 movie entitled "Gaslight." That's not to say that narcissists and gaslighting never existed until after the film, of course. In the movie, a man brainwashes his wife into thinking she is losing her mind. Whenever he used the gas lights in the flat above, his wife would notice that the lights in their own home would go dim. However, he would continually make her believe she only imagined things.

One of the saddest things about being a victim of gaslighting is that it can lead to Stockholm Syndrome, in which the victim begins to look to the narcissist to tell him/her what to think and how to feel, *as well as what reality is.* You even become sympathetic to the narcissist, because you start to think such false thoughts like, "How incredibly frustrating it must be for them to have to put up with my messed-up memories!"

If you're a victim of gaslighting, you may find it hard to see the abuser for who they really are. It's not because you're stupid; it's more likely that the narcissist can charm you out of your mind. They're so charming that you start to feel rotten forever second-guessing them or doubting them. They lay that charm on so thick that you stop trusting your gut and start trusting them. You don't realize it, but you've been expertly maneuvered into an unhealthy and abusive relationship.

Now, let's look at some of the ways that the narcissist messes with your gas lights without you knowing.

Classic Gaslighting Tactics and Effects

Reframing. This is when the gaslighter reframes or twists whatever happened so that it sounds like they were the good guy, or that they were the victim in the whole thing - and you're the villain. This makes you wonder if you're wrong about what you thought their intentions were. They will often reframe along with insincere compassion, which just adds to the feelings of irrationality and instability that you already feel. For instance, if the abuser hit you and you know for a fact that they meant you harm, they can say, "Oh come on, I didn't hit you that hard! It was only a bit of fun roughhousing. Stop making a big deal out of this."

Switching subjects. The narcissistic gaslighter will choose to change the topic rather than address the questions you're asking them, or the point you're making. They'll often say, "No, you imagine that just like you imagined the other thing. Did that friend of yours fill your head with her silly ideas again?" Now, they've made it about the friend they don't like, rather than focusing on the issue at hand.

Downplaying. The gaslighter will make your feelings and thoughts seem inconsequential, to the point where you start asking yourself why you're always so touchy about things. The more they can make you feel inconsequential, the more power they will have over you.

Denial. I once overheard a conversation between two teenagers at the mall. One of them had been in trouble at home and was telling the other about it. She said when her mother found out, she did the only thing she knew she could do to get out of trouble. In her words, she said, "Deny, deny, deny, until you die." It sounded like a mantra the way she said it, and I've been unable to get it out of my head ever since.

Denial is a classic gaslighting tactic that the narcissist uses. You know that they said something or did something; you bore witness to it with your own eyes and ears. Despite this, they deny it. Sometimes, it's not even because they didn't realize you saw them; they know you saw them do what they did. However, they will blatantly deny it. It is this denial that confuses you. It's only natural to wonder if your mind is working right because normal people would not bother pushing a lie when they know they've been caught in it.

Not the gaslighter. They have no problems going as far as asking you to prove what you're saying is true. This is a classic example of gaslighting, because in certain situations, all you have is your recollection of events. As such, you may start to wonder if they're right and you're wrong. Maybe you're the crazy one, you assume.

Outright Lies. It isn't just that the narcissist tells bald-faced lies that leave you in shock, it's also the ease with which they lie that is disturbing. They're very comfortable with it. These lies promote "crazy-making," presented so smoothly that you begin to wonder if you're not a bit nuts for not believing them.

Killing you Softly. A good narcissist has the intention of making you into a shell of who you are. You may not notice as that more they gaslight you, the more you give in and become someone you don't recognize anymore. They kill you - ever so softly - ever so slowly, erasing the person you really are and leaving behind a puppet that they can play with however they like.

Using your Treasures Against You. Do you love your job? Your children? Your pet? The abuser has no problem using whatever you hold near and dear as a weapon in their gaslighting techniques. They are adept at making you come to the assumption that you do not deserve the nice people or things in your life. You find yourself questioning why you have it good, and if they've done their job right, you will sabotage all the relationships and accomplishments you hold dear.

Love Bombing. The reason gaslighting works so well as a manipulative technique is that the narcissist conditions you into being okay with abuse by using the carrot and stick method. When they sense they've laid on the lies, denial, and unjust punishment too thickly, they will follow that up with a whole lot of love and flattery. A perfect example is a man who beats his wife only to buy her diamonds or the woman who cuts down her man only to make him his favorite meal, or generously entertain his friends only because she senses she's pushed him a bit too far and just might lose him. The narcissist will use love and flattery to keep you around for more abuse. The sad thing is that you get used to constantly being sad and abused. When they're loving and flattering you, you think to yourself, "Well, they must not be as bad as I thought. I don't know why I got mad. I'm staying."

Are You Being Gaslighted?

It can be difficult to tell if this is the case, on account of how badly the abuser may have messed with your psyche at this point. I have compiled a list of questions you need to ask yourself so that you can figure out whether you are the victim of gaslighting:

1. Do you often ask yourself, "Why am I so sensitive?" all through your day?

2. Do you find yourself constantly making apologies?

3. Do you feel like you're a bit nuts, continually confused in your relationship with this person?

4. Do you have a constant, nagging sensation that there's something wrong with your relationship, even if you can't put your finger on it?

5. Do you keep wondering why you're not as happy as you know you can be?

6. Do you find it challenging to make even the simplest of decisions?

7. Do you find yourself making an excuse after excuse for the way your partner treats you?

8. Do you find yourself constantly feeling like you'll never measure up or be good enough for your partner?

If you answered yes to these questions - and you're not dealing with low self-esteem, depression, or anxiety disorders - then you're most likely being gaslighted by this person or the specific people who make you feel this way in your life. Observe your interactions with the people in your life and notice the ones with whom you constantly feel these things. If you only ever feel that way with a person or group of people, it's likely that you are a gaslight victim.

Chapter Four: How Gaslighting Affects Your Mind

Gaslighting is a terrible thing, as it can lead to severe mental health issues for the victim. Having to live each day in confusion and self-doubt is more than enough fuel to feed the ravenous fire of anxiety. Also, as a victim of gaslighting, the constant feeling of low self-esteem and utter hopelessness can cause depression, as well. In addition to anxiety and depression, it is not uncommon for victims to develop unhealthy codependence and Post Traumatic Stress Disorder.

Gaslighting is clear emotional abuse. Don't take it lightly, and don't assume simply because you now know what it is (or that you call your partner out on it) that that will be the end of that. That's hardly ever the case. Anyone who would deliberately, consistently make you doubtful of your sanity and memory is a toxic person who is not going to change overnight just because you've shown them the error of their ways.

Gaslighting is an abusive, manipulative technique that is so powerful; it can badly affect your mind. You become very destabilized and unable to think for yourself as clearly as you're used to. *Over time, this self-doubt becomes so intense that you find yourself starting to look to your abuser for clarity, direction, and purpose.* You're probably already thinking about it, but gaslighting is not just something that happens in interpersonal relationships. It also happens in the field of politics by unscrupulous politicians who want to make sure they keep the balance of power on their side.

In the beginning, gaslighting seems like a simple disagreement. You feel like there's nothing to it. However, to be able to spot it for what it is, you should notice that the abuser has a habit of lying all the time and constantly denying the truth - *even when there is evidence of it.* They'll also continuously engage in misdirecting you or the topic at hand, and they will contradict themselves as well.

Gaslighting and Mental Disorder

The very first time gaslighting was clinically observed was in 1969. The report showed that, in several cases, the only reason some patients wound up in a mental hospital was that someone (or some people) had hatched a devious scheme to make them seem mentally unwell. This is gaslighting in its purest form, where the goal is to make you look and feel insane so that you can be totally removed from the equation. It's not always this extreme, though. For the most part, abusers engage in gaslighting just so that they can keep you under their thumb.

Sandra is a great employee who is great at what she does. However, for some reason, her immediate superior makes a point of constantly leaving her out of meetings. Magically, his memos never get to her. She's approached him about it, but he keeps waving her off dismissively, telling her she's only paranoid, and she's probably losing the memos because she never keeps her facts straight.

Antoine finds himself the continuous victim of his father's verbal and emotional abuse. Every time he does speak up about it, his father tells him to "man up" because he's way too sensitive, "like a girl."

In both of these scenarios, you can see clearly that it's only natural for the victims to begin questioning their own perception of reality, and with this continued abuse, it's only a matter of time before Sandra believes that she's no longer as sharp as she used to be, and Antoine buys into his dad's narrative that he needs to stop being so sensitive.

How You Are Affected by Gaslighting

It's one thing to talk about gaslighting and narcissists, but it's another thing entirely to talk about them from the perspective of you. Let's look at the various adverse effects that gaslighting can have on you and your mental wellbeing. After all, the narcissist is like a leopard unable to change its spots. The most important factor in the gaslighting equation is not the narcissistic abuser, but you and your feelings.

Typically, when you're in a narcissistic relationship, you will find yourself feeling constantly unsettled, anxious, and worried. You feel an air of hopelessness, and you are mired in a state of learned helplessness. You're constantly walking on eggshells around this person, saying sorry more times than you care to count, asking yourself if you're right, doubting yourself, and swimming in confusion. You find that the things you used to really love doing no longer make you happy, and no matter what you do, you just never feel good enough. Then there is that unspeakable feeling of shame and guilt that isn't and shouldn't be yours to wear around your neck. You feel emotionally and mentally exhausted.

Battling feelings of doubt. The reason your confidence is completely ripped to shreds is that the narcissist begins their work *from within,* and over time the doubt really seeps through everything you do. Whenever you're trying to connect with someone who is unable to pay attention or care, and who constantly has nothing but challenging questions for you, you begin to ask yourself these questions as well. You buy into the lie that you're incapable of handling yourself. To add fuel to the fire, you feel helplessly stuck in this relationship, fueling your self-doubt even more.

You've likely read blogs and books, most of which tell you the sad truth: the narcissist is never going to change. You get that in your head, but your heart is another thing altogether. Not unlike the narcissist, you begin to buy into fantasies of your own. "She will change," you tell yourself, refusing to leave, caught in the addiction that they have created in you. You might even be able to see when others are being gaslighted or manipulated in their ways in their relationships, but you tell yourself that your relationship is different. You try all sorts of things, but you realize over time that you have no control. Your narcissist holds all the cards, and you just can't walk away for some reason. This doubt eats its way into other aspects of your life, including your career, family, and friendships.

Never feeling good enough. It doesn't help that we've all been taught that with enough blood, sweat, and tears, we can make anything work. This may be the case in other aspects of life, but it is not so with the narcissist. You find yourself thinking, "If I could only be better, then they would finally love me as they used to in the beginning." Deep down, you probably know you'll never be good enough for them

It feels like they're always on the lookout for your slip-ups — never mind that those slip-ups shouldn't even be considered *in a healthy relationship.* They never notice anything you do right and are quick to lay down the law and make you feel bad the minute you step out of the invisible, constantly moving line they have in their heads. The more you try and fail to be acknowledged for it, or fail to better your relationship with this dementor, the more you feel inadequate and begin to blame yourself. In extreme cases, you lose your very own identity. You no longer have a clue who you are anymore. Keep in mind that it isn't that you're not more than enough. You are. You're just dealing with a narcissist, a bottomless abyss who will never be filled no matter how much of your soul you give.

Swimming in a sea of confusion. Today, you're the center of their attention. They lavish you with sweet words, gifts, praises, belly rubs, all the good stuff. Tomorrow, they're cold and distant. They disappear without calling. They go off doing whatever they want to, and you have no idea where they are or who they're with. It's like you don't exist. When it's great, it's great. When it isn't, it really isn't. Also, things just keep ping-ponging from bad to good and back between the two of you. Naturally, all of this leaves you feeling very confused about where you and your relationship stand! It's not your fault. Your narcissistic lover is just very inconsistent. It's the nature of the beast.

It wouldn't be so confusing if they had always been cold and distant from the get-go. You would have been able to take off and leave before things got too serious between you two. However, this person makes you feel like they know the essence of you. You feel like both your souls are so intertwined. They make you feel that way, telling you you're the best thing to have ever happened to them. Yet, they'll keep you under wraps from the people in their lives, and they won't bother to show up for you when it really counts.

The reason you feel confused is that an abuser is an empty person whose attention stays on whatever they find most interesting or useful *now.* If that means lavishing you with sweet nothings, then they'll do that. If they suddenly find something more interesting, then they're off. You're basically an object to the narcissist. You're nothing more than a supply for them. When they say they love you, it's not *you* they love; it's the way you *make them feel.* Any "love" shown disappears as soon as they find something else that makes them feel alive. When that thing is boring, they're off to the next thing. The only reason you become convinced that the gaslighter loves you is that they have charm and charisma for days – more than enough for you to make something out of their sweet nothings.

A constant stream of apologies. Along with the self-doubt that plagues your psyche, is the frequent apologizing, even when you don't have to or shouldn't have to. You should only apologize when you're in the wrong. You can also say "sorry" when you notice that something else has made someone disappointed or sad, in order to show empathy. For instance, you can say, "I'm sorry for your loss." It's obviously not your fault; it just shows the other person you care about their pain.

However, when you're dealing with a gaslighter, you'll find that "I'm sorry" is your new anthem. It doesn't take much for you to disappoint them since they're so entitled and love to keep others on their toes. You'll begin to apologize for every little thing, fueled on by your doubt. You chorus endlessly, "I'm sorry... I'm sorry..." because you have learned that no matter what you do, you will never be able to give your significant other exactly what they want.

Sadness, anxiety, and depression. Not only do you feel anxious and depressed on account of the helplessness you feel in the relationship, you feel that way also because the gaslighter is not one to reciprocate your emotions. You find that you're constantly sad and down, you're not interested in doing anything that you used to find fun, you're plagued with guilt, you feel worthless, and you often withdraw from all social interactions. It's difficult for you to sleep, and you adopt poor eating habits as well. In this depressed state, you're unable to deal with the gaslighting properly. Your spirit is completely broken at this point.

Gaslighting also causes severe anxiety. When you feel like you cannot sort out your relationship or get it back on track no matter how hard you try, your anxiety builds, and sometimes grows to full-on panic. You feel your heart racing. You're unable to breathe right. You get dizzy spells. You're overcome with the feeling that something bad is going to happen soon.

Thankfully, both anxiety and depression can be treated. All you have to do is see a professional psychotherapist who can help you work through all you're feeling, give you constructive tools to move past the abuse and gaslighting, and prescribe you the required medication to help you get better.

Learned helplessness. Over time, when you've had no choice but to keep enduring situations which you'd rather do without, you find that you're unable and sometimes unwilling to do anything about your predicament — even when you have the power to put a stop to it. This concept is called "learned helplessness" and was developed by the University of Pennsylvania's Martin Seligman. You learn that there's nothing you can do about the problem, and so you keep tolerating it. Even when you finally have a chance to escape it or put a stop to it, you don't. This is not your fault. You've been taught by the gaslighter to feel helpless.

Gaslighting can lead to learned helplessness, thus increasing the likelihood that you will suffer depression and apathy. When you've been the victim of gaslighting for long enough, you learn to accept that that's the way things will always be. You grow passive about your life, never bothering to challenge your abuser. You know logically that you can walk away, but because you have been taught to stick things out so that they can get better, you stay. You buy into the ideas that if you try harder, you can make things work between you both.

A loss of pleasure. One thing that happens a lot with people who suffer at the hands of gaslighters is a complete inability to enjoy things that would ordinarily give them pleasure. You may have found that ever since things went downhill in your abusive relationship, you no longer enjoy being with people you love to hang out with, and you don't care much for that Taekwondo class you were so excited about. Your life moves from color to black and white, and you do not feel any drive to do anything anymore. If you can sum up everything you do feel, it would come to just two words: Why bother? On account of the dissatisfaction you feel in your relationship, you no longer enjoy life's simple pleasures. That dissatisfaction bleeds out from the relationship into other aspects of your life, and you quite literally stop caring.

Overwhelming shame. The sad, horrible thing about shame is that it only leads you to more bad choices. Your gaslighter is simply unable to deal with the shame that they feel on the inside, and that makes them do the most questionable things. When you try to hold them accountable for their actions, they will only respond by raging out and doing something worse. How does that affect you?

You know when you've done something that you should be ashamed of. However, you own it, learn your lesson, and move on, resolving not to repeat such shameful behavior. In other situations, you might wall yourself off from other people to avoid judgment, or because the shame is eating you alive. It's like talking about how healthy your food choices are when you know that you snuck out to the grocery store at 2 am for some chocolate bars (which you chomped on in secret, of course!)

Over the course of your relationship with the gaslighter, you start to feel shame as your family and friends begin to point out that the abuser treats you is simply unacceptable. You might feel ashamed about the way that you're being treated, and the fact that even if you know better, for some reason, you keep letting it happen. You're also ashamed because you feel people are judging you for staying instead of moving on with your life. This shame hits you from many angles. The next thing you know, you're avoiding all contact with the very people who can help you escape. You grow weary of lying to others that everything is fine with you and your gaslighting significant other. As you isolate yourself from people who have your best interests at heart, you find that you leave yourself more vulnerable to the gaslighter, just as they want it.

Emotional and mental exhaustion. Being in a relationship with someone who gaslights you is exhausting. You don't know understand what's going on, and you burn a lot of mental energy trying to work out what the deal is with this person who claims to love you. You're drained emotionally, because it's like every new day (even every new hour) brings a new struggle. You feel like you keep having the same arguments and the same conversations endlessly. There's no change, no matter how seemingly sincere they sound when they say they'll try to do better.

This exhaustion dulls your mental faculties so that your performance at school or at work is not quite what it used to be. It drains the quality of your other relationships as well, leading you even deeper into isolation. Long story short, the psychological dangers of gaslighting are very real and very detrimental to your life - in all aspects.

Chapter Five: 30 Phrases Gaslighters LOVE to Use

Stuff Your Gaslighting Abuser Says

If there's one thing I've learned from interacting with people who have had to battle being with a manipulative gaslighter, it's that without fail, the abusers all seem to have certain choice phrases that they all use. It's almost like they all graduated from Gaslight University or something. Here's what your abuser will say:

1. You're only acting this way because you're so insecure.

2. You're too sensitive!

3. Stop being paranoid.

4. It's really not a big deal.

5. I was only kidding!

6. You take things too seriously.

7. You're acting crazy right now.

8. You know you are a little nuts, right?

9. You're just making all that up.

10. Stop being so hysterical!

11. Can you be any more dramatic?

12. You're so ungrateful!

13. That's all in your head.

14. No, that never happened.

15. You're lying. No one believes you. I'm not buying your nonsense.

16. If you had just paid attention.

17. We've already talked about this. Don't you remember?

18. Don't you think you're maybe overreacting?

19. If you had just listened.

20. You keep jumping to the wrong conclusions.

21. You're the only person I've ever had all these issues with.

22. I'm discussing, not arguing.

23. I know exactly what you're thinking.

24. What does it say about you that that's what you think?

25. The only reason I criticize you is that I'm looking out for you.

26. Don't take every single word I say so seriously.

27. You need to get better at communicating.

28. Calm down.

29. You're overthinking this. It's really not that deep.

30. What if you're wrong again, just like the last time?

Think about the context in which you hear these phrases being said to you. Were you talking about sex? Family? Money? Habits one or both of you have? You'll notice that these phrases often pop up when the conversation is centered upon that.

It's a sad truth that, for the most part, the victim is a woman, and a gaslighting narcissist is a man. The reason for this polarization of genders in narcissism is that, often, women have learned to doubt themselves and to apologize whenever there's a problem or disagreement with their significant others. Men, however, are not socialized this way.

Examples of Gaslighting

Scenario 1: Mark and Jeanine are a couple who have been together for some years now. In the beginning, Jeanine never realized she was dating a narcissist who continuously discredited her in her absence, making her look bad to her friends and family. Jeanine had wondered for the longest time why it seemed like her loved ones were distancing themselves from her. One day, she had a heart-to-heart conversation with her sister's best friend, Ruthie, who told her that the reason everyone was weird with her was Mark had told them that she constantly abuses him, verbally, and physically.

Meanwhile, Mark had the proof: He went as far as sending himself emails using Jeanine's account, scalding himself with hot water every now and then and then sending photos to her family for them to see what fresh hell Jeanine had supposedly wrought on him. Meanwhile, whenever they came around, he would be the doting, loving husband, making her family and friends resent her even more for something she didn't do! Jeanine would cry to her husband often, bemoaning her fading friendships and relationships, and he would comfort her, telling her it was all in her head, that they still cared for her, and she was only paranoid.

Scenario 2: Amy had always had a very rocky relationship with her mother, Lucy. Her mother had abused her terribly growing up, every time they were left alone at home. Lucy would make Amy stand in a tub while she poured scalding hot water into the bath, hurting Amy terribly. She would tell her all sorts of hideous things, like, "You're good for nothing, Amy. All you ever do is ruin things."

Meanwhile, when others come around, Lucy is the perfect mother. Fast forward to Amy being a grown-up now. She decides to confront Lucy about her constant abuse and does so. Amy is shocked at the response she gets from her mother. Lucy simply says, "None of that ever happened. You just imagine things. You know you were a kid. All kids at that age are stupid. You're no exception." No matter how much Amy pleaded with her mother to own her wrongdoing, Lucy denied it all - even raging about it. Amy resolved to end her relationship with her toxic mother and never discuss the matter again since it was clear she was not about to get an apology for the years of abuse, let alone an acknowledgment that it happened.

These are very real examples. I've simply changed the names to protect the identities of the people involved. That said, there are thousands and thousands of horror stories about gaslighting being shared every day on the Internet. It might seem like it's an easy matter to cut the manipulator off simply, but is it, really? Can you break free with no consequences or damage to your psyche? Let's find out how gaslighting affects your mind in the next chapter.

Chapter Six: Signs of Gaslighting

Before now, we have briefly touched on various signs of gaslighting. In this chapter, we're going to pay more attention to what gaslighting looks like in various scenarios, from your most intimate relationship to family, work, the media, and politics.

What Gaslighting Looks Like in Relationships

Gaslighting happens a lot in romantic relationships. First, the gaslighter will love-bomb you. This is called the idealization phase, where you're their one and only, and you could never do any wrong in their eyes. They will give you all the love you want and then some. Often, the narcissist will move way too fast and has no problems pursuing you relentlessly, getting you hooked on all the love and attention which they will only take away in the devaluing phase. Once they have you wrapped around their finger, they withdraw all that love which they've got you hooked on at this point. You'll do anything to get it back because you know that they've loved once, so if you try hard enough, maybe you can get them back. It won't happen, though. They'll start to treat you badly, instead. This is where the gaslighting comes in as they start with the lies, cheating, and violence, making you think it's all in your head, and you're nuts. In severe cases, you can have a nervous breakdown. There have been countless cases where gaslighting has led to suicide.

First, come the lies and exaggerations. What they do to you is to create false stories about you to make you look and feel bad. It's all set up to make you think that there's something about you that's just plain wrong. These stories are propped up by lies, accusations, and untrue assumptions, not facts that you can verify. This way, you're instantly forced to get on the defensive. For instance, a wife can say of her husband, "He was a terrible father, and I had to let him know that." A father can say to his daughter, "I hate it when you wear those off the shoulder tops! I've told you before: you look like a slut!" A manager could say to an employee, "You and your position are dispensable. I don't even know why we're still keeping you on."

Then come the repetitions. These lies and exaggerations need to be repeated often enough so that the gaslighter can keep you on the defensive, which allows them to dominate your relationship with each other, and dictate how all conversations go between you two.

Escalating in the face of a challenge. Did you just dare call the gaslighter out on their vicious lies? Then it's time for them to escalate! You'll never hear them acknowledge that you're right, and they lied. They will simply double down on their lies. Do you have evidence that they are lying? Good for you! Unfortunately, the evidence is only useful in a court of law. They will deny everything, blame you, and pile on more and more lies, bring in an issue that has nothing to do with the problem at hand, say stuff that makes others doubt you, add in more sauce to make you doubt yourself, and leave you in a tangled mess of confusion and frustration. "I moved in with my mother briefly, because she said she was depressed and needed company. When I moved in, I began to get sick. I don't fall ill that easily. One

135

day, I walked into the kitchen and saw my mom putting rat poison into the pasta we'd just made together. She flat out denied it. I pushed, and she said she just keeps some spice in the box just as a gag. I acted like I bought her story. The first chance I got, I took that box and compared it to another from the store. I also went to get checked out in the hospital. My mother had been poisoning me in little doses."

Bring on the exhaustion! The gaslighter will keep attacking you nonstop until you feel completely worn down. At this point, you're so discouraged that you're resigned to your fate as a victim. Your happy self is gone, replaced by this fearful, pessimistic, self-doubting, self-loathing person. You're in a state of debilitation, wondering if you can trust your own perception, no longer able to recognize yourself, no longer sure who you are and what you want out of life.

Now comes the codependence. Now, you're in an even worse place in your relationship. You've become excessively reliant on your abusive partner for emotional and psychological support and guidance. You notice at this point that you are riddled with feelings of anxiety and insecurity, leaving you at the mercy of your abuser. Only they can give you the acceptance and approval you seek. They alone can make you feel safe, secure, and respected, as far as you're concerned. The gaslighter giveth and the gaslighter taketh away, and there's not a thing you can do about it. You have become vulnerable. Fearful. Codependent.

A dose of false hope. There will be times when the gaslighter will be kind to you. They will treat you better, one way or another. However, it's really all for the show. You find yourself thinking, "Well, they're not as bad as I thought. I wonder why I ever thought they were terrible to me. Perhaps things can be better. Let me give this another chance." Aha! They have you right where they want you! The sudden change of heart is that it's all part of their manipulation to make you let your guard down and put you at ease. It's to dissuade you from taking any action to free yourself. Once the gaslighter notices that you've calmed down a bit, they will get right back to attacking you.

136

This constant push and pull are how codependency and learned helplessness develop.

Dominate and instill control. The goal of the gaslighter is simple. It's to dominate, control, and milk others for what they are worth. By keeping up with the threats and lies, the gaslighter makes sure that you constantly feel afraid, in doubt, and insecure. When you feel this way, you're more vulnerable and open to them taking advantage of you whenever and however they like, all for their own selfish ends.

What Gaslighting Looks Like in Family Relationships

In some families, gaslighting is a very real thing. A lot of kids, sadly, are victims of abusers who gaslight them into anxiety and depression. Here are some of the more common ways gaslighting shows up in families:

- **Contradictory and Unpredictable Parenting:** As a child in a dysfunctional home, nothing is predictable for you. Chances are one, or both parents are hooked on alcohol or other drugs. They're here today, and not the next. Your parents' moods tend to oscillate wildly, no thanks to whatever substance they abuse. If they made plans with you, those plans are going to be dead in the water. Even in moments of calm, you can't truly relax because sooner or later, something will upset the balance, and things can quickly get intense, even violent. When you grow older, you don't rely on reading body language to understand people, because you have learned not to trust it. You don't know how to deal with your own emotions, because you never had a good role model for that. You don't trust yourself, and you most certainly don't trust others either.

- **Push and Pull Parenting:** In this case, one or both of your parents probably struggled with Borderline Personality Disorder or schizophrenia. As their kid, they always put you in a double bind. Today they love you to an uncomfortable point that you might as well say they "smothered" you. Tomorrow, they push you away, coldly. What you feel as a kid is that you're nothing of consequence. You feel like you don't matter. You grow into an adult who does not trust themselves and must always look to others for a sense of validation. Your life feels surreal and out of your control. You are anything but self-reliant, and you want to look to others for help, but you don't know how to ask for it.

• **Appearance-Based Parenting:** If you grew up in a family like this, then appearance is everything. Your parents insist that you all present a united, picture-perfect front — even if it's really hell to be a part of this family. You're not allowed to make mistakes. You're not allowed to feel. What you're supposed to do is make the family look good. *It's tasking and draining, and it's no fault of yours.* Chances are you've been saddled with narcissists for parents who simply do not do well with being perceived as flawed. You have no choice but to fall in line.

• **Emotionally Indifferent Parenting:** As a kid, your emotions are ignored. To your parents, emotional needs are not a thing. You've got a roof over your head, food to eat, clothes to wear, and they expect that that is the be-all and end-all of parenting. You never got any attention or care whenever you showed emotion. Each time you cried, one or both parents told you that you were too emotional or too sensitive. You learned to hide your emotions. You learned to keep it all inside and keep a stiff upper lip. Growing up, you have issues connecting with others because you don't open up. You feel numb. In extreme cases, you could become a sociopath or a narcissist when you're an adult.

Here's a general overview of what it's like to be gaslit in a dysfunctional family:

Your sadness is dismissed. Rather than acknowledge that you're going through something, your folks choose to tell you there's no problem to begin with. This is confusing for you, because you know there's a problem. You feel sad! You feel hurt! If there were no problem, surely you wouldn't be feeling this way. Instead, your parents tell you that you should never cry — especially if you are a boy. This is the worst thing to do to a child. There is no set rule for how and when to experience your feelings. When you're told not to cry, you feel like you're invalidated. You feel like none of your reasons for feeling the way you do are valid. You feel like you don't matter.

Your likes and dislikes are dictated to you. Your parents love to tell you what you like, and what you don't like. It doesn't matter that you prefer a good book over television. It doesn't matter that they constantly see you trying to read. They'll still insist that you like TV. They will dictate what your preferences are. Essentially, they take away your power of preference, so that no one ever gives you what you really want.

Your imagination is often mocked. You may have had your parents call you nuts for sharing some subjective experience you had. Or it can even be a real thing you saw, and rather than pay attention, your parents will tell you your imagination is running wild again, or that it's all in your head. There's that gaslight again!

Your ideas are dismissed as silly. It's sad that a lot of parents — even the ones who are well-intentioned towards their kids — will often tell their child that their ideas are silly. This tends to happen a lot because of the age difference between you and your parents. Just because you don't agree with your parents on something does not mean you're ignorant; abusive parents make that assumption all the time. They will tell you that you're naive, or you're a rebel. The fact is everyone is entitled to their opinion, no matter how old or young you are.

You're wrong, and they're right — and they don't need evidence to prove it. Every time your parents often dismissed you, saying you're wrong and they're right. All they need to be right is the fact that they're older. This isn't to say that every time someone tries to show you where you're going wrong; they're gaslighting you. However, if it so happens that even after they invalidate your decisions, you're right more often than not, then you're most likely being gaslighted.

You call them out on their shortcomings, and they hit you with denial and outrage. The right thing to do when you hurt someone apologizes, no matter their age, status, race, or whatever. You might not have meant to hurt them, but you did, so you should apologize. However, that's not the case with your abusive parents. They'll deny they did it or tell you that you're the one responsible for your feeling and their actions had nothing to do with it. A good, loving parent knows they need to attend to their child's emotions, not have an intense argument about whether their child should feel how they feel.

What Gaslighting Looks Like at Work

The gaslighter at work is one of the most indignant people you'll ever meet. When they're saying shameful, untrue things about coworkers, or bosses, they will do so with complete conviction. If you didn't already know them for the evil demons they are, you would completely buy into their lies. You say something to them about it, and they ignore you. They carry on like you never spoke. Insist on being heard, and they will change the topic, or argue you into submission, or make it seem like you're making a big deal out of nothing.

The effect of being gaslighted at work is that you find yourself doing all that you can to prove yourself to them. It feels like if you're not careful, you'll be out of a job. You suffer from added stress and anxiety, wondering when you'll become the target of the gaslighter, worried about how to protect yourself, even as you keep contorting yourself into impossible shapes to please the gaslighter. You're always on the defensive, and probably depressed, as well.

The trick to dealing with the workplace gaslighter is to have support systems in place, *outside of work* with family and friends.

Also, make a habit of documenting every interaction you have with them. It may seem extreme, but keep that recording app easy to access on your phone's home screen, if you can. Do your best to speak with other coworkers who are also having issues with this character and see how you can all work together to make sure no matter what the gaslighter does, there is always a witness. Here's how you feel when you're being gaslighted at work:

You always get backhanded compliments from the gaslighter. You get compliments like, "Wow, I'm surprised you can actually do that. Well done!" Or "Coming from you, that was not so bad actually." You know you did well, and yet you feel badly when you hear compliments like that.

You constantly feel confused every time you interact with them. No one is right all the time. However, if you always doubt yourself whenever you're dealing with a certain coworker, wondering if you're actually any good at your job despite the evidence you have that you really are good, then you're probably being gaslighted by them. You feel confused about your thoughts and abilities every time you interact with them. This is no accident, as the more confused you are, the more the gaslighter has room to be right about everything, or at least feel that way.

You don't feel you're worth anything. And it's all because of them. You suffer from a bad case of imposter syndrome, where even though you're a pro at work, you still feel like an incompetent fraud who will be found out eventually. This is because that gaslighting manager or coworker makes sure you always feel like you're doing a poor job. If you're not careful, this feeling of incompetence can spill over into other aspects of your life. You're going to need to set up very clear and strong boundaries so that you can protect your self-worth and sanity from your workplace dementor.

You get no validation or empathy from them. In healthy human interactions, there is always some form of validation. When you're dealing with the gaslighter, the validation is completely missing. You don't get the sense that you can safely share your feelings with this person and be understood. The gaslighter couldn't care less about your feelings. They won't bother with them. In a situation where you want to explain yourself, the gaslighter does not want to hear it. They are incapable of giving you the benefit of the doubt.

What Gaslighting Looks Like in Politics and the Media

Gaslighting is very prevalent in the media and in politics. As much as we'd like to think that the media is completely objective, these days, it very clearly isn't. Everyone, on every side, has an agenda that they are pushing. When the media decides to get behind someone or to stand against someone, they also engage in their own form of gaslighting as they share their opinions, which are not always backed by facts. This is especially the case when it comes to sensationalized news.

In politics, there is a lot of gaslighting that goes on. Politicians make false claims all the time so that they are not held accountable for their actions or inactions, or so that they can sway the people however they want to. In fact, you don't have to look very far to find times when certain politicians have said things live on the air, and despite the videos that go around proving they really said what they did, they say it never happened! They never said it like that! They accuse the media of editing clips to make it look like they're the big bad guy. While the media does engage in such manipulation tactics as deliberately skewering clips to make them seem a certain way, this is not always the case.

The political gaslighter, when completely backed into a corner and forced to be accountable for their own actions, will offer a backhanded apology at best. They will say things like, "The words I used do not reflect who I really am as a person." That's just a fancy way of telling the public, "What you just witnessed and observed was all in your head and didn't happen the way you clearly saw it did."

Chapter Seven: How Narcissists Choose and Test Their Victims

You must have wondered endlessly how you could ever be a target for the narcissist. You're a good person who does not deserve to be treated so terribly, after all. What is it about you that attracts the narcissist? What is it about you that makes them say, "Aha, there's a good target to lay all this evil on"?

It is no fault of yours being chosen as the narcissist's target. They just happen to be the most efficient and deadliest of emotional predators. They know the best people to target, and you're not a random choice. They're not targeting you because you're a terrible person, so don't assume you're broken.

Things about You That Make You a Target

You're a caring, loving person who is passionate about helping people. At the beginning of your relationship, everything seems nice and beautiful. However, that changes quickly. At the beginning of your relationship, if you're a giver, you'll naturally want to give more and more to your significant other. The thing about the beginning of love is it works great for the narcissist, as they get to be your one and only. All your attention is on them all the time, and they love it, being the emotional vampire that they are. As time goes by, the narcissist sucks you dry, insidiously gaining power over you without you being aware of what's going on.

You've got something the gaslighter wants. It can be your lifestyle. It can be money, position, or power. Whatever it is, they want something from you. Your relationship probably began with the narcissist being ever so helpful. However, the second thing doesn't work out for them, they take away the carrot, and you get the stick. The second it becomes obvious to them that you now know what they're really after and it's not you, they'll just escalate the tension that's already there. The narcissist wants only one thing from your relationship, and that is complete control of whatever it is they perceive you have.

You had a dysfunctional childhood. If you had the misfortune of growing up in a dysfunctional family, then it can make it hard for you to notice when you're being abused, or when your boundaries are being disrespected, since that's all you've ever really known anyway. You probably also have trouble setting boundaries, and when you do set them, you're probably not firm about them. For this reason, the narcissist is drawn to you. They're not a fan of boundaries. Therefore, they choose you so that they can exploit this weakness of yours for their own selfish purposes. As part of their abuse, they will swoop in and do everything for you. On the surface, it seems like they're incredibly helpful, but what's really going on is that they are creating a situation where you can't do anything for yourself. You come to depend on them for everything. Their helpful heroics only serve to take away all sense of empowerment and independence from you.

You have compassion and empathy in spades. Nothing is ever the narcissist's fault. There's always something or someone else responsible for their misfortune in life, as far as they are concerned. As you listen to their sad tales, you find yourself drawn in, wanting to help them in some way, since you are compassionate and empathetic. This works for the narcissist because they become the center of attention in your world. Inevitably, what starts off as a good intention on your part becomes an unhealthy, life-sucking relationship in the end.

You keep accepting blame for stuff, even when it was clearly not your fault. In your steadily worsening relationship with the narcissist, you will find that they're always covertly or overtly saying that you're the problem. They'll shift the blame onto you and pile on the guilt as well. They will say, "Well, if you hadn't acted the way you did, then I wouldn't have gotten upset." So rather than having the focus be on the horrible thing that they did to you, they've shifted the blame onto your shoulders by saying it was your fault they acted that way in the first place. They'll dig their heels in too so that you cannot get back to the topic at hand.

You're lonely and desperate for love. The narcissist always seeks out people who have a deep need that needs to be taken care of. They love knowing that you need friends, or you need to be loved, and will more than happily fill that role. In the beginning, you might assume that their intensity is a good thing. You might assume it is a pure passion! However, that's not the case. Over time, the intensity tapers off and does so drastically. The warm and loving narcissist is suddenly cooler than the arctic, detached as a stranger. This leaves you confused, wondering what you did wrong and how you can fix it, just so you can get back the person who once held the brightest, hottest torch for you.

You run the other way when it comes to conflict. If you make a habit of avoiding confrontation just to keep the peace, then this makes you a prime candidate for the narcissist to target. Often, people who are not confrontational have a very deep fear of guilt, abandonment, and the end of relationships that matter to them. When the narcissist rages out, you feel this fear in you become active, almost crippling your ability to think straight. You will do whatever you need to in order to keep the peace; the more you run from confrontation, the more the narcissist is drawn to you.

How the Narcissist Tests You

Each time you allow the narcissist to get their way in the beginning, you don't realize that you're being tested. This is one test you absolutely want to flunk! The way to flunk is to stand your ground, assert your rights, and not be so agreeable or flexible.

It is one thing to know that - at some point - the narcissist has tested you or will test you. However, that doesn't help much if you can't even recognize when you're being tested. Let's look at some of the "tests" set for us, so we can fail, and fail excellently every time!

The narcissist tells you that they'll call you by a set date and time, but then they don't. This is not random. It's a test. What happens after that missed appointment is that they will eventually get in touch with you and act like everything is fine and dandy when it isn't; you've been waiting for your phone to go off when they said they'd call, but it never did. Now they're talking to you as if there's nothing wrong at all as if they never promised to call when they asked you to. You're left feeling like an anxious mess! What's the goal? They want to see how you take it. They want to know how you react. They will have some very convenient excuse, saying something popped up or they forgot, but that's no error. They deliberately chose not to call because they needed to read your reaction. If you call them out on it, they will accuse you of acting out too strongly. Note: this is not to say that every time this happens, you're dealing with a narcissist. If you call someone out on that, they will genuinely apologize if they didn't mean to do it. However, if you're talking to a narcissist, they'll be upset that you're making this a big deal. That said, if you know someone who keeps doing this, then you should cut them loose; they aren't worth your time or effort.

The narcissist asks you to change something about yourself or the way you look. Say you just met, or you just got into the relationship, and then your significant other tells you to change something about the way you like to dress, or the way you do something. That can be a possible red flag! No one in their right mind would tell someone they just met, or only just started dating to change this that and the other about themselves. Whatever you do, be yourself. Don't assume, "Well, this relationship will be for the long haul, so let me change what they want." Don't do it! Be yourself, and if they're not a narcissist, they'll be completely okay with you as you are.

The narcissist overshares about their terrible exes and terrible childhood. This is also a test to see how you choose to respond to their tales of woe. As they share, you'll notice them also probing you with questions about your own childhood as well. Now, there's a chance the narcissist really was abused or had it rough growing up. Of course, that's a terrible thing, no matter who it happened to. With that said, be on your toes, because they might be looking for your weak spots as they try to create some *cognitive empathic connection* with you. They just want to know what makes you go soft and weak; eventually, they can use that to their advantage. The first time you meet someone is not the best time to talk about your dark and terrible past or the trauma you've gone through. That's not a healthy start to a relationship or friendship.

The narcissist says, "You can trust me," when you've both only just met. The thing about people that cannot be trusted is that they are likely to use the phrase "You can trust me" when you just met each other. They would not even be discussing such sensitive issues that require trust when you're just meeting unless you're in group therapy or something. There is a natural sequence of events when it comes to relationships and friendships. The last thing you want to do is accept that statement at face value and open up because you just might be dealing with a narcissist. If you open up, they will assume it's easy for them to get into your head, and they will have a lot they can use against you.

Sometimes There's No Reason

There are times when you become the target of a narcissist, not because of anything in particular, but simply because you happened to be in the wrong place at the wrong time. Don't assume there's something wrong with you because they chose to target you! There's a little something called transference which narcissists are guilty of. It's when they take their rage or anger and direct it at the closest, most convenient, most reachable person that they can bully... and sometimes, you're it!

Whatever the case may be, know that you are your own person. You don't have to be a victim. I was in my 30s before that I realized I didn't have to keep taking abuse from others. Coming from a dysfunctional home, I had no idea what boundaries were, and what was not okay. However, I learned over time, and since then, my life has been free and clear of narcissists. When I do encounter one, I find that I value my freedom and joy too much to let them make my life horrible. I would love for you to find this same freedom and joy, too. If things have already gone too far that you don't even think you can set yourself free, then please see a professional therapist to help you find yourself again.

Chapter Eight: When a Gaslighter Accuses You of... Gaslighting!

Here's an interesting thing gaslighters: They will accuse you of doing the very thing that they're doing! The gaslighter finds a way of working things out in their heads so that as far as they're concerned, you're the manipulative psychopath. This manipulative tactic of accusing the gaslighted person of gaslighting is deviously brilliant.

As you already know, the whole point behind gaslighting is to invalidate you and your experiences, make you look bad, keep you uncertain and unbalanced, and have you wondering if you can trust your version of events. These are things the gaslighter does either to get vengeance or to get total control over you.

You're familiar with the usual shenanigans from gaslighters, including outright lying, lying about what they did and didn't do or say, regardless of the fact that you remember it differently, painting you as unstable and crazy to others, getting people to join them on their crusade against you, and also putting you and your friend or family member at loggerheads with each other.

A lot of gaslighters will often project their guilt, shame, and wrongdoing onto their victim. In fact, if you want to know what the gaslighter has been up to lately, all you must do is pay attention to whatever it is they're accusing you of. The gaslighter could be an addict and have no qualms accusing you of being one - telling your friends those same lies. They will cheat, come back home, and accuse you of doing the same. They will manipulate you and accuse you of being manipulative. How in the world do you keep up with that? You feel overwhelmed, and who can blame you?

Why does the gaslighter accuse you of gaslighting? It's simple; pure projection, or a pre-emptive strike.

Projection

The reason the gaslighter accuses you of gaslighting them could be because they're projecting. This is something they do in self-defense. They are unable and/or unwilling to own up to their terrible behavior. Rather than be held accountable, they put it on you instead. Sometimes, they understand they are projecting, and that is usually the case when they're trying to get something they want. Other times, they're very unaware. Regardless of which case it is, this is very unhealthy and abusive. You should never stand for that.

There are gaslighters who do not realize that they are driven to project because they feel a burden of shame or guilt. Typically, as far as the narcissist is concerned, they're fine. They're perfect. It's everyone else who has issues. This is one of the reasons it's hard to encourage the narcissist to seek professional help since they're flawless as far as they're concerned. There are, in fact, cases where the narcissist truly believes their own stories. They truly believe you're gaslighting them when that is not the case at all, and they are the one gaslighting you!

I need you to understand that no matter what spurs the narcissist on to project their terrible behavior onto you, all the blame and shame and guilt is theirs to bear, not yours. Don't waste your time trying to straighten them out, or defend yourself, because there's just no changing their minds.

The Pre-Emptive Strike

Let's look at what's really going on when the gaslighter accuses you of gaslighting as a pre-emptive strike. Say the gaslighter is cheating on you, meeting up with their lovers secretly, and loving it. They will do anything to keep up the illusion of them being loving partners to you. So, they accuse you instead. After all, they're the faithful ones, and you're not.

Besides keeping up that illusion, gaslighting you by accusing you of cheating keeps you so busy trying to prove you're not - and so torn up emotionally - that you are unable to spend any energy or time observing that the gaslighter's own behavior is off. They will go as far as they need to, just to keep you off track, even claiming they saw you at some hotel with someone, even if they know you weren't. It is quite a difficult position to be put in *since there's no way to prove something that isn't happening*. Even if you do manage to get a camera set up on you along with a tracking device 24/7, it still will not be enough for the gaslighter to believe you.

Want to know how much further the gaslighter can go in gaslighting others into thinking you're the actual gaslighter? Well, let's look at Melissa and Andrew. Melissa has no qualms manufacturing evidence that she's being manipulated by Andrew, whether it's by withholding some facts or twisting them entirely out of context. Andrew told Melissa he would have to be out of town for a week because of a work conference. He had religiously called her every chance he could get so that she'd know he was always thinking about her. Meanwhile, back at the ranch, Melissa is telling all their friends that she's very sure Andrew is off with some waitress from their favorite restaurant, cheating on her. She tells them that he said he'd be taking a work trip, but that the last time he said that, she found out he was sleeping with "some other floozy." On and on, she would go, fabricating more and more reasons she is sure this work trip is just him cheating on her.

Mario and Nelly are another couple dealing with gaslighting. Mario loves to use cocaine. He's addicted. Countless times, he has stolen money from his girlfriend, Nelly, to feed his habit. However, before she can ever confront him about this, Mario tells Nelly in the sincerest, most concerned voice ever, that he is concerned about her drug problem. Nelly, confused, immediately jumps to her own defense. It's a ridiculous accusation; she knows for the hardest drug she's ever had in her whole life is wine! The sheer ridiculousness of the accusation shocks Nelly, throwing her for a loop. From her facial expression alone, you would think that Mario would stop there; it's obvious he is lying. What does he do instead? He doubles down on the lie, listing fictitious times and places where he had seen her using the stuff. He says, "You are losing track of time, blacking out, and unable to remember your own filthy, disgusting habit." Nelly began to question her perception of reality. Mario just kept stealing from her and feeding his habit.

Another way the gaslighter does a pre-emptive strike is by using social media. They have a lot of power since when you put something on social media, it tends to spread like wildfire. Rather than the truth, they will post something that makes them look like the saint or the martyr, while you read like the worst villain ever. Add in the appeal of having people accept social media posts at face value, and you can see why the narcissist uses this as a weapon, too.

The next time you're being accused of something by the narcissist, don't react, don't take it personally. Step outside of yourself in your head and look at the situation from a bird's eye view. Ask yourself,

"What is this person trying to tell me about who they are or what they are up to right now?" The answer will come, and it will be clear. Asking yourself this question helps you in your resolve not to engage the manipulator when they gaslight you, but to simply walk away. Don't give them self-defense. Don't explain. Don't tell them they're lying. Just laugh, shake your head, and walk away.

Chapter Nine: How to Avoid Falling for a Gaslighter

Now you know why the narcissist acts the way they do, and you know why they pick their targets. You know what to expect from the gaslighter, and you completely grasp what gaslighting behavior is. A critical question remains: How do you make sure you never fall for the gaslighter ever again? You may have found yourself always getting into relationships with this kind of person. How do you put the kibosh on that, once and for all?

Steps for Protecting Your Heart from the Gaslighter

Don't be in a hurry to reveal personal information. When you're tempted to share, ask yourself this: Would I feel okay telling my colleagues at work? If the answer is no, then just don't do it! You see, when you share private stuff, it often does a couple of things.

First, it makes you feel like you, and this person has some intimacy going on. It makes you feel closer to the person you're sharing the info with. Narcissists know this, and therefore, they do all they can to get you to open up, so they can speed up the process of getting close to you. You should never let people get too close until you know the sort of person that they are.

Sharing too much too soon also leaves you vulnerable to the narcissist. They can use what they have learned about you to attack you. You will wish with all your heart that you'd kept your mouth shut when you're dealing with a narcissist.

The truth is that we all love the feeling of intimacy. It is this craving that makes us so willing to reveal stuff to others, especially when they've just laid themselves bare, too. There is nothing wrong with intimacy. Just make sure it happens only with people you trust. That, by default, means people that you've taken enough time to get to know.

During your initial conversations, ask as many questions as you're being asked. When the narcissistic gaslighter is probing you, you don't know - at the moment - which you're dealing with. The best way to be safe is to ask them just as many questions as they're asking you. Always wait until you get an actual answer. If what they say is very vague, then ask a more specific question.

Why does this matter? Narcissists will keep trying to draw information out of you. They move hard and fast so that they can learn all they can. When you ask them questions as well, you keep the playing field level. You get to learn about them, too, whether they want to let it out or not. Even their silence or shiftiness can tell you all you need to know about whether to move forward with this person. Also, as you ask questions too, you'll slow them way, way down.

For instance, if you tell them you're a fan of creamy alcoholic drinks, and they hit you with a "Me too!" you can follow that up with, "Really? What's your favorite bar?" Or you can ask them which kind of said creamy drinks they love the most. This follows up question will box them into having to be specific. In the process, it's not hard to tell if they're lying, since the more specific they must be, the more they will falter. This can also throw them off and make it less likely that they continue engaging with you. That's a win! Always more and more questions, even as they do. Reciprocity is a huge part of any relationship.

Keep your private time private. At the beginning of your relationship, you might notice that you're being bombarded with so much "love." You're not! The only reason you're getting all that love and attention is that the narcissist knows this is a very good way to control you. When you become accustomed to being the center of their universe, they immediately withdraw all that affection. What you should do in response to all the calls, messages, and texts, is nothing. Let your time be yours. Do not reply until you're good and ready to. When a narcissist always calls and texts you, it's no accident. It's a good way to keep you disconnected from those who really care about you and center your attention on them instead.

The narcissist needs attention. When they bombard you with all those calls and messages, they are trying to feel you out and see if you'll give them all the attention and narcissistic supply you need. When you don't give them what they want, they will have no choice but to give up on pursuing you. If someone really and truly cares about you, they will respect your privacy. They will understand that your time is yours to do with as you wish. They will not seek to eat into the time you could spend working on your own projects or building other beneficial relationships as well.

In the beginning, do not make the mistake of fighting for the relationship. Let's say you only just started dating this person, and they're already telling you that their family and friends do not approve of you or the relationship, or they tell you that they will be leaving town soon, or that they are concerned that you'll break up with them. All of these are red flags. What they're prodding you for is your word that you will never leave them. There's nothing wrong with seeking assurance, except that you've only both just started dating; *it's way too*

157

soon for that. If they say something that indicates to you this relationship will crash and burn in no time, just get out.

When you date a narcissist, it's not unlike getting interviewed for a job. The narcissist wants to make sure you will rough it out with them for the rest of forever — however long forever is for them. They want to know that no matter how bad things get, you will do everything within your power to make sure that you both work as a couple. There's nothing wrong with all of this when your relationship has been going long and strong for a while. However, when you start declaring your undying devotion to early in the relationship, it tells them that you're desperate. Desperation is a weakness that they will not hesitate to exploit once they sense it in you. They want someone who is way too desperate to simply get up and get out of the relationship, no matter how bad things get.

If they know they would have to leave town, then why bother dating you, to begin with? If they are bothered by the fact that their loved ones do not approve of them being with you, then why bother continuing the relationship? A lot of the time, all of these seeming stumbling blocks don't exist. The narcissist is simply trying to get you to make a commitment. The thing about decent people is that when they commit or make a promise, it takes a whole lot to get them to break that promise. This is the one time it's okay to not stay true to your word. The narcissist is not worth losing your sanity and peace of mind over! If the narcissist gives you the impression that there is a lot keeping this relationship from lasting long, then see it for what it is: they are pressuring you to commit too much, too soon.

Keep Your Private Space Private. Don't be in a hurry to let someone move into your home immediately. You may have been in a situation where "just one night" became several months or years. When this happens, it is a major red flag. Do whatever you need to do in order to make sure that they don't stay at your home.

Why does this matter? That kind of major move is exactly what the narcissist does to control the way your life goes. The next thing you know, they are in your home and a part of it, just like furniture. The longer you let them stay, the more stressful it is when you need to keep your space as you'd like it to be. Don't be in a hurry to let them move in. You must first figure out your priorities, and then figure out where your relationship fits in. It's not unusual to love having other people around. After all, a good company is always great! However, the best friendships and relationships do not depend on spending a lot of time together over a short period of time. It's about respecting one another and honoring the other person's priorities as well.

Maintain your previous friendships and keep pursuing your hobbies and interests. If you're dating someone who must be with you every minute of every day, then this is not loving. This is not normal. It's a clear sign that something isn't quite working the way it should in their head. It's way too early to want to spend so much time with someone at the beginning of your relationship.

They start digging for too much detail. You can tell them you love clubbing with your friends, but then they might begin pressing you for more details, like, which friends? Which club? What time? How long will you be there? When you notice this, don't give them too much info. It will drive them up the wall — and as far from you as possible.

Understand that this is important because the narcissist does not want to share you with anyone. They want to have you completely to themselves. That's why they work tirelessly to cut you off from the people who love and support you. It's for this reason you need to keep engaging in hobbies that have you meeting new people and keep hanging out with your friends as well. If all you have in your life is the narcissist, then you will inevitably depend on them for all your social and emotional needs, and this means surrendering your power to them!

In a healthy relationship, your partner will respect the time you spend with others, and not ask you every five minutes via text when you're coming home. They will allow you to live and have some fun. If you think that you need to respond to that text, or you need to call it a night because they've said they miss you five times in a row, understand that it's not that you're a good lover; it's that you have been trained to obey. Break the chains!

Don't take care of people you only just met, no matter how badly you want to. If you notice that there is someone in your life who has hit a rough patch in life, and you feel the urge to help them out, take a moment to ask yourself why. Also, ask yourself if it's plausible that there's no one else they can look to for help. Do this all the time, no matter what. Here's why: You might be dealing with a narcissist who is trying to get as close as they can to you by putting themselves in a seemingly vulnerable position in your eyes. This way, you feel compelled to step in and be their savior. Do that, and they've gotten you right where they want you.

They can have very valid reasons for why they have no place of their own, or no job, or no money. With that said, you don't have to play Superman to their Lois. You don't need to save them because they just got out of an unhealthy relationship. Don't be the rebound! Move on. It will be difficult because you're in a battle against your natural instincts, which are to help others who are helpless get back on their feet, take care of them, and do whatever you can to help them grow. However, a relationship is only healthy and worth being in when it involves two individuals who are both able to take care of themselves without any help. If you get into a relationship where one person cannot take care of themselves, or shoulder some of the load, then where do you think this is going? Nowhere.

Notice the way that they treat others when you're out on a date. Pay attention to how they treat everyone, particularly people who must serve them. As you observe, put yourself in the other person's shoes and ask if you'd be okay with being treated that way.

The classic narcissist feels like there is nothing wrong with making others around them feel small. They honestly believe that they are greater than everyone else, and as such, it's okay for them to treat others poorly. This is not okay! You might want to excuse it because they're so nice to you, but I've got news for you: This is the same way they will treat you eventually. You'd best get up, thank them, pay for your part of the tab if you've already started on dinner and drinks, and walk away. You want to date someone who respects everyone, no matter who they are or what they are.

Don't get into planning the rest of your lives with someone you only just started dating. Don't be in a hurry to agree to move to France and getting a little cottage with a white picket fence just yet — not when you've only just begun the relationship. When they start with those plans, don't be afraid to say, "I think we're moving way too fast." It's okay to say this! Be honest. If they really love you, they won't have a problem with you telling them that you need to take things slower with them.

The narcissist will pressure you any way that they can to keep you very committed to the relationship. When they start mapping out a future for you both, make no mistake that they're doing this so that later on in the devaluation phase, they can remind you that you committed to making it work and that you committed to their plan. They will get you to fall in line by making you feel guilt and shame for not keeping your word, even though your word was given way sooner than it should have been before you had all the facts on this reptilian masquerading as a human.

There is anything wrong with making plans and having dreams of the future with your significant other, but it should take a fair bit of time to get to the point where you are one hundred percent sure you want to commit to this person for the long haul. Don't let anyone rush that process for you.

Always reciprocate. Did they give you a compliment? Give them one as well. Did they ask you a question about yourself? Then throw them a question of your own, too. The reason you should always reciprocate is that balance is important in a healthy relationship. When you treat someone the same way that they treat you, you can use your own feelings as a barometer of sorts to figure out whether or not the way they're treating you is normal, or if it's a waving red flag.

For instance, if someone constantly bombards you with gifts, then attempting to do the same thing will help you see what's really going on. You can see past the rush of receiving gifts, straight to the intentions behind them. There are some generous people out there who have no hidden agenda, but you just must be careful. If they're always complimenting you, do the same thing to them. You will be able to tell at some point that you're no longer sincere in your compliments, and you will then sense that something is off about them.

Typically, dating a narcissist will change your whole life. The key is to be aware of this change as it happens so that you can pull out as soon as you can without losing yourself. Armed with this Intel, you now know what to do to avoid getting sucked into dating a narcissist who will completely ruin your life indefinitely. Don't feel bad if a lot of relationships you get into don't last as long as you'd have liked. Be glad instead that you get to come out of it stronger, wiser, with a clearer picture of who you are and what you want for your love life.

Chapter Ten: Dealing with Gaslighting: Dos and Don'ts

I promised at the start of this book that this would be unlike any other book on narcissists or gaslighting that you've read before, and I meant it. You are going to get the tools that you need to deal with the thorn in your flesh that is the narcissist.

Ideally, the best thing to do is go no contact, ditch them, and just leave. That's what a lot of books advocate, anyway. This advice, however sound, is sometimes just not practical. Sometimes, you just can't leave. You wonder if there's a way to make them change so that your life is a lot more manageable. It can be that the troublesome gaslighter is your manager, and you need to be on their good side, or you'll lose your job or get a slash in pay. It can be that the gaslighter is your significant other, and you've got kids, and you're not ready to disrupt the life the kids are comfy with.

Well, you'll be happy to know that there are other solutions besides simply running for the hills! You can't stop a narcissist from being a narcissist, but you can help them improve. Don't tell them that, though. They are flawless, like Beyoncé. Remember? So how exactly can we deal with these gaslighting devils?

A Little Bit of Sympathy

I know what you're probably thinking. "Wait. What?!" Hear me out, though. Narcissists can use some sympathy because we all, to one extent, have some narcissistic traits of our own. The difference is that with the narcissist, these traits occur in the extreme. These are traits that are good to have to certain degrees. If they didn't exist at all, we'd be living on a little blue dot full of low self-esteem.

Narcissism exists on a spectrum. Things only get worse the further down you go, where you've got the evil narcissist with the overly entitled attitude and zero consciences when it comes to exploiting others, being dishonest, and all that other horrible stuff.

To get deeper into this "a little bit of bad is good" line of thought, let's look at grandiosity. The fact is it's great for feeling happy, fulfilled, and healthy. A wee bit of narcissism in your adolescent years is also great because it allows you to survive all that usually accompanies that stage of life and living. Even as a teenager, it helps to be moderately narcissistic, as you have a smaller chance of suffering from depression and anxiety, and the quality of your relationships is significantly better than your self-aware, non-narcissistic peers, or your overly narcissistic ones. The surprising benefits of moderate narcissism do not just stop in school. It can be a big help when it comes to your career. The bosses who are a bit narcissistic are often seen by their employees as being better at getting things done when compared to the overly narcissistic or non-narcissistic leader. In other words, the only difference between the malignant narcissist and us is where we fall on the spectrum.

When narcissism is on the furthest, malignant end of the spectrum, that's when it becomes a disorder. The only way that you can be of any help when it comes to making the narcissist a better person is to recall that this is a mental issue. In the heat of the moment, this is not an easy thing. All we can think of is the fact that this person is terrible. However, when we've been able to get away from their clutches, put some distance between you and their toxicity, and allowed ourselves to heal enough so that we can stand on our own two feet, we need to recall that just like we would show sympathy for sufferers of anxiety, borderline personality disorder, and depression, we should do the same for those with narcissism.

No Love

One common thing about most narcissists' childhoods is that they were never given true love when they were kids. They never knew the security of being shown, unconditional love. They were never shown any appreciation for simply being their authentic selves. Their parents and others in their lives only ever celebrated them when they achieved something. They never received any empathy, and on account of this, they learned to be distrustful of everyone. They learned to become ashamed of their authentic selves and to hide that self away.

Put yourself in the shoes of the narcissist like a child. Having tried and failed unsuccessfully, you decide that you're done trying to fulfill your emotional needs. You're done hoping you'll be loved for simply being you. The goal becomes apparent: You need to be more special than others. You need to do better than others. You've got to look better and be smarter. You choose to stop looking to people to help you feel validated, and instead, you focus on being the best at everything you do. You imagine a world where you are far better than everyone around you. Why am I having you look through the eyes of the narcissist like a child? It's simple: this is where the key to helping them lies.

Fixing Perfection

Let us revisit the issue of empathy when it comes to narcissists. As I've mentioned before, empathy is something they are not quite used to working with on their own. It's a muscle they've never really had to flex for most of their lives. While the psychopath is a narcissist, the narcissist is not necessarily a psychopath. They can feel some empathy if they try. You can help them learn how.

If you resort to name-calling or criticism, all you do is make them even worse. The narcissist will simply resort to being more of what you hate. However, when you help them remember that relationships matter, in the most compassionate way that you can, you can help the narcissist in your life to do better.

This is not wishful thinking. Studies have shown that simply teaching the narcissist to be more compassionate and caring is enough to reduce their narcissistic traits to somewhere near manageable if they are approached in a soft and gentle manner. The more you reflect secure love to them, the more they become comfortable with being loving and committed to you.

To fix your perfect narcissist, you don't berate them because of their many achievements, or their drive. You don't make them feel bad for having achieved so much. You don't criticize them for being manipulative and callous when it comes to other people's feelings. What you should do instead is let them see first-hand how it pays to be more understanding and to be willing to work well with others.

I ought to warn you that while this does have amazing results, you're not going to see changes overnight. They won't suddenly swing from being terrible and unpredictable to loving and stable. You'll need to give it time and use a very special technique.

Empathy Prompts

The way to reduce or get rid of narcissism is to use empathy prompts. First, you need to speak up about how your relationship is important, and then you need to speak up about the way you feel.

When you talk about why your relationship matters, you must make sure you use statements that are affirming and supportive. Tell, "I care about you deeply," or "You mean so very much to me," or "You're very important to me." When you use these affirmations, the narcissist gets the message that they do matter to you. They feel something they've not felt in a long time, if ever. They feel reassurance. As you use these affirmative statements, you will find that the narcissist will slowly but surely move from thinking about you and them as separate from each other, to think about you both as a team. They also get another message: They can get secure, safe, unconditional love from you.

You can say to the narcissist, "Look, I feel like you're one person who matters the most to me in the world, so it really hurts when you're always suspicious of me. It makes me feel like I have failed you." You can say, "You're more important to me than you know. That's why it hurts when you refuse to return my messages and calls for days and even weeks."

Note that empathy prompts only really work with people who display narcissistic tendencies! If we're talking about someone with a clear case of Narcissistic Personality Disorder, you're probably not going to get very far without enlisting the help of a licensed psychotherapist. Don't let this get you down, though. You can still use empathy prompts to see if there's any hope at all when it comes to the narcissist in your life. Just make sure you are very sincere, and you don't raise your voice when you use the prompts. Also, don't covertly guilt trip them. If you do this right, you will notice that your narcissist will soften up.

Signs That Empathy Prompts are Working

If you want to be certain that they're working, look out for the following responses from the narcissist:

- They'll want to clarify things. They'll do this by asking you questions like, "For how long have I been making you feel bad or sad?"

- They'll affirm you. In response to your empathy prompts, they will say, "You matter to me too. I don't want ever to hurt you." or something to that effect.

- They will validate your feelings. "I know, my sarcastic comments hurt you deeply."

- They will also apologize. "I'm sorry. I never wanted you to feel sad."

Note that all of this works great when you're dealing with your narcissistic lover. You most likely won't be getting this intimate with your manager or colleague at work.

The Narcissist at Work

Open any book, and they will most likely recommend that the only way to deal with the narcissist at work is to report them to the relevant authorities and get them fired. However, that just doesn't work as well as these books want you to believe they do. Research has shown that a measly 1.7% of such abusive cases get investigated, and lead to the abuser being punished accordingly. In 6.2% of the cases, the abuser is dealt with, but the target is not protected in any way. In 8.7% of the cases, the matter was investigated very unfairly, and there was no punishment to keep the abuser in check. 31% of these cases were never thoroughly investigated; there was no fair play, no punishment for the abuser, and a lot of punishment for the target. In 12.8 percent of reported cases, nothing was done, and the matter was simply ignored, with no punitive measures for either the target or the bully. In 15.7% of reported cases, nothing was done, but the target experienced retaliation from the abuser for reporting the matter while the target remained employed. Finally, in 24% of reported abuse cases at work, the employers simply fired the targets. What do all these stats mean? Reporting the abuser works only about 30% of the time. There's a 70% chance that you'll be the one run over when you do choose to report.

Dealing with the Workplace Narcissist

Reward the narcissist for good behavior. When the narcissist does something good, compliment them. When they act warmly, praise them for being warm — not for their performance at work. Only ever praise them when they show some sort of empathy or human kindness. Always be on the lookout for the chance to compliment them on being a more caring, cooperative coworker who cares about other people's happiness. Always compliment them when they act like a team player.

Work using the word "we" as often as you can. Use it every chance you get. Whether it's an email or a memo, always put the word everywhere you can. It might seem like it would be a complete waste of time, but there was a study conducted that showed the more narcissists encountered the words "we," "us," and "our," the more they were open to helping others around them, and the less they cared about getting fame and fortune. So, let us make this a brand-new habit we use to our benefit!

Teach them about effect, behavior, and correction. You first begin by telling them how you feel. This is the "affect" bit of the equation. When you share your feelings with the workplace narcissist, tell them how you feel. This means you'll be using a lot of "I" statements, like

"I'm feeling uncertain/unhappy/uncomfortable with this." Don't go for stronger sounding emotions like afraid, depressed, or scared, as you're at work. Stick with the less intense words like in the example I just gave you. The point behind this is to talk strictly about your experience. This means you're not going to use the word "you." Don't say, "You're making me feel uncomfortable." Say, "I feel uncomfortable."

Next, you move on to the behavior. This is where you let them know what' causing you to feel the way you do, whether it's an action they've taken, something they've said, or an experience you have had. So, you'd say, "When you only criticize me," or "When you don't let me speak," or "When you yell at me."

Finally, we move on to the correction. This is the change in their behavior that you would like to see. To be able to assert your desire for these changes, you simply must request for them. You're going to tell the narcissist what it is they must do in order to make your interactions with each other work better. For instance, you can say, "Can you be kinder when you're showing me where I went wrong?" or "Can you allow me to finish sharing my thoughts with you?" or "Can you speak more softly?"

Here's how the affect-behavior-correction or ABC technique would play out:

"I feel really unhappy all through the day when you yell at me in the presence of everyone. Can you give me feedback in a softer tone and only one-on-one?"

Make a clear contrast between good behavior and bad behavior. Have you noticed that complimenting the narcissist is making them do better? Then you can rev things up a bit by contrasting their bad and good behaviors. Be careful with this, as you want to be diplomatic here, not start World War III. The way to do this is to talk about both the bad behavior and good behavior at the same time. If you really want to effect change, then it is better to compare the two with the narcissist, so that they can clearly see how acting as a team is better than shooting people down. You can say, "It was so much more productive during our meeting last week when we let everyone have their say. Today's meeting wasn't really like that. Can we try to do the next meeting like last week's?"

A Summary of Dos and Don'ts for Dealing with the Narcissist

Do stay defiant when it comes to protecting your sanity and standing your ground about what you know to be your true and valid experiences.

Don't agree to change your reality to suit the narcissist. You know what you know. Your experiences are valid. You know the truth.

Don't allow the gaslighter to bully you into letting go of your truth.

Do acknowledge and accept that you will never get accountability. The narcissist will never own their wrongs. They will never tell you you're right. They will never be logical or reasonable with you. Know this, and you will no longer feel powerless.

Do let go of the desire for things to be different. When you desire for things to be different, it keeps you blinded to the fact that reason and logic can never work with this person.

Don't hold the narcissist to their empty promises. They will tell you that the abuse will never repeat itself, but it will. It always does.

To create a healthy form of detachment from the gaslighter. This means you need to be able to tell the difference between the real world and the fantasy that your gaslighter has conjured for themselves.

Do write down your experiences, which validates what happened for you so that no matter what the gaslighter says, you know what's real.

Chapter Eleven: 7 Ways to Stop a Gaslighter in Their Tracks

If you've read up to this point, then chances are you're probably thinking of a long list of people that have just got to be narcissists or gaslighters in your life. However, as a caution: Not everyone is a narcissist just because you have a little tiff here and there. Also, keep in mind that you might be recollecting past events through the narcissistic glasses, and so everyone might seem to be that way.

With that said, if you've asked yourself the questions listed in this book, and have observed for yourself that you really are dealing with a gaslighter, how do you deal with them? Let's get into that.

Putting an End to Gaslighting

Pay attention to the pattern. One of the major reasons gaslighting is so effective is that, for the most part, the target is completely ignorant of what's happening. The minute you move from ignorance to complete awareness, you will have successfully taken back some of your power. You will find it easier to shrug off the narcissist when they start playing games again.

Keep in mind that the gaslighter might never change, no matter what you do. Sometimes, the only way there can be any change is with the help of a professional. Gaslighting is all that the manipulator knows how to do, so you cannot expect them to give that up in favor of logic or reason. There is no other better coping mechanism that they know. This is not to say that they should not be held accountable for their actions. I'm just making sure you now not to hold on to the hope that they will change. They could, but don't hope for it. Accept that they're wired the way they are, and only professional therapy can help them become better people.

Remember that gaslighting behavior is not necessarily about you. It all really comes down to the fact that the gaslighter needs to feel like they're in charge. They need that rush of power. At their core, the gaslighter is riddled with insecurity. The only way they know how to get rid of that feeling is to make others feel less than they are, or at least give themselves the illusion that they are better than everyone else. Keep this in mind, and you will not bother internalizing anything they say or do anymore. You will be in a better position to manage the relationship you have with them or to end it altogether.

Create a support system that you can rely on. Dealing with a gaslighter on your own is no walk in the park. It helps to have other people that you can talk to, who will validate your perception of reality as well as your sense of self-worth. If you've noticed that ever since you got involved with the narcissist, you've somehow been cut off from the people that matter to you, then now is the time to reach out to them. Do not buy into the narcissist's lies about how no one else can love you the way they do. That is simply not true! Commit to spending time with your friends and family. Make appointments, if you must. Treat these appointments with as much commitment as you would a business meeting. The less isolated you are, the less of a hold the gaslighter can have on you.

Spend a long time thinking about whether you want to keep investing in the relationship. This is crucial, especially since having to deal with the gaslighter's shenanigans eats away at your peace of mind, self-worth - and even your health. Is the gaslighter your manager, or your boss? Then take proactive steps to find another job, making it a non-negotiable agreement with yourself that you're moving to a different, better job. If the gaslighter is your lover and you'd like the relationship to continue, then keep in mind that you'll both be needing some therapy, and you will have to make that a non-negotiable aspect of your relationship if you decide to stay.

Start to build your self-esteem back up. Having been with a gaslighter for too long, it's easy to forget just how awesome you are! You need to take some time to remind yourself of everything about you that is amazing, no matter what the gaslighter has said to make you think otherwise. You might need to begin journaling so that at times when you are low or starting to buy into the insidious lies they have packed your head with, you can reopen that, and remind yourself of your awesomeness. Don't just write about the great things about you. Write about times when you felt the most alive, the most joyful. As you do this, you will naturally find yourself craving those times again, and taking action to liberate yourself and your mind.

Be open to getting professional help. It's difficult being the victim of gaslighting. Your self-esteem, sense of self, and sanity will have taken a beating. You might find that you're slow to make decisions, constantly unsure of yourself, and always wondering if you're good enough. You might even be suffering from depression or anxiety. If you find that you're overwhelmed by feelings of helplessness, uncertainty, hopelessness, and apathy, then chances are you need to seek the help of a professional psychotherapist right away, so that you can rebuild yourself after the devastating damage caused to you by the gaslighter.

Chapter Twelve: Can a Gaslighting Narcissist Change?

Everyone wants to know if the narcissist is capable of change. You're not alone. It's a valid concern for so many reasons. For some people, they're so invested in the relationship with their partner that they don't want to believe all the years were for nothing. They don't want to believe that they've been holding on to false hope for so long. You probably know how that feels. You got into a relationship with your partner with an open heart and mind, not expecting anything beyond love and acceptance. Over time, you learned that they were never really who you thought they were. Even if you know this, for some reason, you just won't let go. You believe if they were loving then, then they can be that way now. Besides, sometimes it really is good, isn't it? You know it probably won't last, but at least it must be a sign that the narcissist can change for the better, right?

Change Is Possible

There it is. The answer you've been hoping for, waiting for with bated breath: it's possible for people to change, no matter what personality disorder they have been diagnosed with. Think of these diagnoses as a shorthand way of describing certain people. You can never use one word to totally encapsulate a person's life. When words like extrovert, introvert, or narcissist get bandied about, they seem to imply a permanence to the individual's personality. That's not always the case.

It helps to consider that these disorders are not necessarily descriptions of who people are in summary. It would be more accurate to think of these labels as the perfect descriptions for behavioral and/or inter-relational patterns, and nothing more. The same applies to narcissistic personalities.

Born of Vulnerability

A lot of researchers are of the opinion that Narcissistic Personality Disorder is a result of growing up in conditions where it's not safe to be vulnerable. The narcissist as a child had to accept that it was a sign of imperfection to be vulnerable, and that showing any vulnerability meant that they had no worth at all. This theory is the reason there's often a connection made between insecure attachment styles and narcissism, meaning the narcissist is driven to control all their relationships because they are afraid to be in a position where they need to depend on someone else.

The narcissist is adept at keeping people from knowing who they really are. They will refuse to acknowledge their vulnerabilities or opt to suppress them or project them onto others so that they can keep crafting the person they want to be in relation to others. For the narcissist to change, they must be willing to be vulnerable. This means leaving themselves wide open to emotions that they have suppressed and denied over the years. The trouble with narcissists is not that they are unable to change, it's that they are *unwilling to* because it would mean that the identity of the person they have struggled to craft will be blown to bits. In a narcissist's mind, all the relationships which they have failed at simply offer more reason why they should remain the way they are.

Understand that the narcissist defines themselves by how others perceive them. A narcissist can't be a narcissist if they don't have anyone to put on a show for. They need to be the center of attention, and so they love to have the spotlight of attention from those who bother to stick around them. Over time, of course, their performance starts to get old. The narcissist knows this and is constantly running scared that others will realize there's really nothing to them. This is one of the reasons the narcissist refuses to change, as they are more certain than ever that the fix is not to come clean and be vulnerable but to put on a more flamboyant show and pile on some more makeup to conceal all their flaws.

When the Narcissist Finds True, Secure Love

When the narcissist happens to find someone who cares about them and is not just sticking around for the flash, they're still deathly afraid that this person will think they're not worth it. The fear they feel is a subconscious one that they are not aware of, but it is very real. This is what fuels the narcissist to do things like shift blame and guilt onto their partner or act all grandiose.

When their antics are exposed to the light of day, and everyone sees them for what they are, they get angry because they've slipped up and alienated everyone who mattered to them. Rather than change their ways, this causes them to double down on who they are. They become even more narcissistic than ever before, ironically leading to the abandonment and rejection that they're so afraid of.

Breaking the Cycle

To help the narcissist, there's nothing else to do but break that vicious cycle. As gently as you can, you need to throw a wrench in the works whenever they try to control you, create distance between you, blame you, or defend themselves. This means letting them know in no uncertain terms that you're willing to have them in your life, but not on those terms. What terms, then? You should show them that they can join you in the sort of intimacy where they can be loved for who they really are, flaws and all. They only need to be willing to let that happen.

The point to take away from all of this is that narcissism is simply one way of relating to others, and you can always change the way you relate with people. It's not going to be easy for narcissists to let themselves get so vulnerable as to allow intimacy, but it is possible.

The Narcissist to who wants to Change

If you happen to know someone who's a narcissist but has expressed the willingness to do better, then you can let them read this section of the book. Here is a list of things the narcissist will need to do to become a better person. ***This is addressed to the narcissist, not the victim.***

Learn to recognize and respect boundaries. When you do, you'll find that you stop losing relationships, and improve them. You must understand where you end, and another begins. You need to understand that other people have their own beliefs, thoughts, and emotions, and they can be completely different from yours while remaining valid. To help you understand boundaries better:

- Listen twice as much as you speak.

- Use other people's names when you write to them, and when you speak to them, too.

- Get curious about the people around you. Ask questions to learn what matters to them and what's new in their lives. Don't be inappropriate in your asking.

- Be mindful of encroaching into other people's personal space and time. Always ask permission first before you do.

- Rather than issue orders, ask open questions. Don't ask leading questions. Don't assume you know better than others.

- When others make a choice that is different from yours, respect it. You won't always get what you want, and that's okay.

Be genuine, always, in all ways. You will find it more refreshing than lying, pretending, and manipulating others. How can you be more genuine?

- Keep your word. If you know you won't keep a promise, don't make it.

- Did you make a promise you can't follow through on? Then own it.

- Don't say or do things that will make others feel like they've been cheated.

Observe yourself often so you can grow in mindfulness. The more you observe, the better you can see how you cause problems in your relationships and push people away. Assume that there's the usual you, and then there's your higher self who observes you from a higher point of view. Here's how to be more mindful:

- Ask your higher or observer self whether whatever you're about to say or do will have good or bad consequences.

- Ask your observer self if your actions and words are all about you showing off, or about you building a great relationship with others.

- Feel like you just did or said something off? Ask your observer self how it would feel if someone said or did that to you. Then apologize and make amends quickly.

Be willing to seek professional help. This will help you along your journey to becoming a more rounded individual, faster. You don't have to struggle with this on your own. You need the guidance of a psychotherapist. You need to be willing to be honest if you're going to make permanent, lasting change. It's going to be so worth it in the end because you will finally discover your authentic self, and your relationships will be better for it.

Do forgive yourself. This is the only way to get the healing you need. It's also the only way that you can be more comfortable with being vulnerable. An added plus is you'll finally be able to flex those empathy muscles. It might be hard to forgive yourself, and you may find yourself crippled with remorse sometimes. Just be kind to yourself in moments like this. You only did the best you knew to do so that you could cope. It's not your fault that you weren't allowed to be your true self when you were growing up. Focus on the fact that now, you can do better. Now, you can rediscover yourself.

Be okay with being human. You won't be perfect. You never were. You have flaws, but that's okay! Learn to be comfortable in your own skin. This is the way to allow rich, beneficial, loving relationships in your life; this is how you grow. You simply need to be fine with who you are. Be okay with being true to yourself, even if it means being vulnerable.

It's going to take you some time. Be patient. You will find yourself. You will also learn that the thing you feared the most is not real. The people who love you don't up and leave just because of imperfection or five. After all, we're all flawed in our own way.

Chapter Thirteen: Exposing Abusive Behavior

You'll get into arguments with your partner every now and then; this is no big deal. That's how relationships work. If you're in a healthy relationship, you'll both go your separate ways, cool down a bit, then come back and try to fix things as a team.

However, when your disagreements start to get abusive, then this is not normal. You know it's abusive when you or your partner begin to act in ways designed to control or overpower you (or another person) whether physically or emotionally. There is the temptation to whitewash emotional abuse by saying, "Well, they never hit me, so I'm okay." However, abuse is abuse, and it is never okay. It's also not happening because it's your fault or you're broken in some way. Please remember that!

The Trouble with Emotional Abuse

The trouble with emotional abuse is that because it leaves no scars, you can see, it often gets dismissed, or is almost impossible to spot when it happens. Make no mistake: the damage from emotional abuse is very real, and it can last a long, long time.

When you're psychologically abused, the other person is saying and doing things to make you think whatever they want. Generally, the goal is to make you confused, disillusioned, and totally dependent on them for your sense of self-worth and identity. It is an incredibly hurtful, despicable thing to do to another person, and can lead to very real mental health issues like depression, Post Traumatic Stress Disorder, and anxiety.

Unmasking Emotional Abuse

There are a lot of myths about emotional abuse, which do a very good job of camouflaging it so that it's hard to detect. Let's rip the mask off, so you can have an easier time figuring out whether you or someone you care about is being abused.

Myth #1: Emotional abuse is always accompanied by physical abuse.

It isn't. There can be emotional abuse with no physical abuse; this often flies under the radar.

Myth #2: Emotional abuse is nowhere near as damaging as physical abuse. This is just pure falsehood. If it hurts, then it hurts. It is not a productive argument to say that one form of abuse hurts more than another. Abuse is not okay. If you're being abused, then you deserve better, and you need all the help you can get.

Myth #3: Emotional abuse only affects women. Abuse can happen to both women and men. There is no exception. Also, it happens in other contexts besides relationships, such as at work, and with friends as well.

What to Do If You're Being Abused

If you're emotionally abused, then you're constantly criticized for everything you say and do. You're blamed all the time, even for things that could never be your fault. You're made to feel ashamed. Your gaslighter constantly threatens to hurt you physically or to do something they know you don't want them to. You feel like you have zero control over your life, as the abuser takes all your power away, sometimes even going as far as controlling your finances so that you have no choice but to stay with them and do whatever they want.

If you recognize yourself in the paragraph above, then you need to do something. You need to reach out and ask for help. There is no shame in that. As a matter of fact, asking for help is one of the bravest things you can possibly do, especially when you're in a situation where you have been completely worn down and out by the abuser.

Reach out for help. It's okay to share how you feel with someone else. You need someone who can make you feel validated. You need someone that can help you to mentally work through everything you've gone through so that you know for a fact you're not crazy. You need someone who can give you hope that your life can get better. If you need counseling, check out https://www.crisistextline.org/get-help/emotional-abuse. You can also send HELLO as a text to 741741, and you will be immediately patched through to a counselor who will help you. Please, be safe. If the abuser in your life makes a habit of going through your phone, then always delete your texts when you send them.

Talk to anyone you can about what you're going through. Confide in them, and not only will you have someone on your side, but you will also be able to occupy your time by hanging out with others besides your abuser. Work on getting more and more people you can talk to who will back you up.

Have a safety plan in place. While there's not necessarily physical abuse going on along with the emotional abuse, it's still important to be safe. This means you need to think up plans for how you can escape from the relationship whenever you are finally ready to up and leave the abuser.

Don't Make Excuses for the Abuse

A lot of the time, people will fall back on mental disorders in order to justify when they do what they do. They don't talk about it like they want to make genuine change. It's just a copout for them to keep treating you the way that they always have.

It's not uncommon for the person abusing you to try to make light of the situation or try to blame you for a reason they're acting the way they do. It can seem like your significant other doesn't know when they do what they do or are completely incapable of realizing the implications of their actions. However, this is just more smoke and mirrors on their part. They know what they're doing. The whole point behind being seemingly unaware is to make you feel even less sure of yourself. Next thing you know, you start wondering if you're not overly dramatic or delusional! I want you to know that your abusive partner is very aware of how they're hurting you, and they always are in control of how they act disorder or no. Want proof?

They will decide when to abuse you, and how far they will push it. A perfect example is when they threaten to hit you but don't. Or when they abuse you in ways that you can never really tell others, because there's no proof, and it can seem like you're making something out of nothing.

They only ever abuse you, not others. If they truly had no control over their actions, wouldn't they abuse everyone in their lives? But they don't, do they? That's because they can control themselves. If it were that they suffered from a disorder, then everyone in their life would get the same treatment, and not just you.

They escalate their terrible behavior. When it's a matter of having a disorder, there can be changes in the person's state of mind. Even then, though, there is a consistency in the way that they behave. However, you may have noticed your abuser will sometimes choose not to abuse you for a while. Other times, they will steadily ramp up the abuse as your relationship goes on. This is more proof that they really can decide to be different or better.

You need to keep in mind that regardless of whether the gaslighter has an actual mental health problem, you are not the one to be held accountable for how they treat you! It's possible to be diagnosed with a disorder and still choose not to act out in controlling, manipulative ways. They will simply need to acknowledge their issues and be open and willing to seek the help that they need. Please, always remember that you're not the reason they act the way they do, and therefore you're not the cure they need. They must own their actions, and they alone can take the first step they need, to change themselves.

If you're being abused, or you're worried about the way your partner treats you, you can also reach out to thehotline.org. To speak with someone, any time, any day, call 1-800-799-SAFE (1-800-799-7233) or (TTY 1-800-787-3224.)

Conclusion

We've finally come to the end of this book; if I've done my job right, you should now have a better awareness of who the gaslighters and narcissists are in your life, and how to deal with them so that you can finally have peace of mind.

I want to stress one more time than if you're the victim of psychological or physical abuse, you must seek the care of a psychotherapist if you can. The dangers of being abused emotionally are all too real and very detrimental to you and your state of mind. There have been countless cases where gaslighting and other manipulative tactics have led to people taking their own lives. I sincerely want to see you thrive and come out of this stronger and better. One way to make sure you don't become a statistic is to seek help!

Make support systems a priority, too. Don't wait to reach out to your loved ones. Do it the very minute you put this book down. Go out for coffee. Catch up. Open yourself up to other people in your life who care for you and want to see you do well. Often, they will be able to see much better than you can, where your boundaries are being violated. They will give you the courage you need to set yourself free from the narcissist and reclaim your power and identity. People need people. That's just the way the world works. Set out to reconnect.

Make new friends. Get back to doing the things you love doing. This will help you when it comes to seeing the real world in stark contrast to the nightmarish fantasy your abuser wants you to buy into.

It can be a bit of a challenge to have a narcissist in your life, *let alone be a survivor.* It can be hard to accept that they just might never change. You give them so many chances, and each time, you know exactly how it's going to go. To protect your sanity, learn to expect that they will revert to becoming the liar, the cheater, the manipulator that they are. Even when they're trying to change, be okay with knowing they will slip up sometimes. With that said, please always check in with yourself. You want to make sure you're living in the real world, and not waiting for that happy ending that will never come.

After your ordeal with the narcissist, it's normal to ask yourself how you ever let that happen to begin with. You wonder what to do with yourself, and if you'll ever find joy. You probably will keep doubting yourself for a bit, wallowing in regret, walking on eggshells when you no longer must. It's okay. Be easy and gentle with yourself. Channel all that energy to your health, your growth, and finding the real you that you'd lost trying to be perfect for the narcissist.

Having gone through the fire, you might feel "done" with love. You might decide that it's best to stop being your compassionate, empathetic self. Don't let this happen! Don't let this one terrible person ruin the goodness of your soul. You are much bigger than that. Do not let someone else's shortcomings dictate how you should live your life. They've already stolen more than enough from you; don't give them anything more! If anything, live bolder, and louder. Channel some of that empathy and compassion you have for others towards yourself, and the next time a narcissist comes your way, you will be absolutely unwilling to settle for anything that makes you feel less than joyful.

It's a difficult thing to do, but you must forgive them in order to move on. This isn't to say forgive and forget." Don't forget, or you'll wind up in the same mess again! Compassionately forgive, but wisely remember. Remember, so that you don't let them in again unless it's on your own terms. Remember how they hurt you, so you do not have to go through it again. Remembering makes you feel powerful because it would be well within your rights to seek revenge, but you're so above it all that you've chosen to forgive and remember simply.

Live, and love with all your heart — and take your brain along with you for the ride. Experiences are great teachers. You've taken a course in Narcissist 101. There's no need to repeat it. If there's one thing you can be thankful for, it's that when you finally reclaim your true self, when you finally break free from the narcissist, you will become even stronger and better for it. You will be able to help others just like you, who are silently crying for help, begging to be seen. I'm talking about those who are hoping that someone like you comes along with a match to ignite a spark in their hearts; so that like you, a roaring fire can begin to burn within them with such intensity that they finally find the strength to set themselves free.

As for the narcissist, don't harbor hate in your heart. Wish them the very best. Wish yourself the same. Then get on with the business of discovering your beautiful self.

References

Alan Rappoport (2005). Co-Narcissism: How we accommodate to narcissistic patients.

Alexander Lowen (2004). Narcissism: Denial of the True Self, Touch stone.

American Psychiatric Association (2013). Diagnostic and Statistical Manual of Medical Disorders–5 (DSM-5), American Psychiatric Association Press.

Andrew M. Colman (2015). A Dictionary of Psychology, Oxford University Press.

Christopher Bagley (2013). Kanye West: The Transformer, W Magazine.

Delroy L. Paulhus and Kevin M. Williams (2002). The Dark Triad of personality: Narcissism, Machiavellianism, and psychopathy, Journal of Research in Personality, Volume 36 (6).

Eleanor Payson (2002). The Wizard of Oz and Other Narcissists: Coping with the One-Way Relationship in Work, Love, and Family, Julian Day Publications.

Elsa Ronningstam (1996). Pathological Narcissism and Narcissistic Personality Disorder in Axis I Disorders, Harvard Review of Psychiatry.

Elsa Ronningstam (2005). Identifying and Understanding the Narcissistic Personality, Oxford University Press.

Frederick S. Stinson (2008). Prevalence, Correlates, Disability, and Comorbidity of DSM-IV Narcissistic Personality Disorder: Results from the W ave 2 National Epidemiologic Survey on Alcohol and Related Conditions, The Journal of Clinical Psychiatry, 69.

Heinz Kohut (1971). The Analysis of the Self: A Systematic Approach to the Psychoanalytic Treatment of Narcissistic Personality Disorders, University of Chicago Press.

Jean M. T Wenge and W. Keith Campbell (2009). The Narcissism Epidemic: Living in the Age of Entitlement, Free Press/Simon & Schuster.

Joel Paris (2013). Psychotherapy in an Age of Narcissism: Modernity, Science, and Society, Palgrave MacMillan.

Martin Seligman (1972). Learned Helplessness, Annual Review of Medicine, Volume 23.

Otto Kernberg (1975). Borderline Conditions and Pathological Narcissism, New York, NY: Aronson Press.

www.ingramcontent.com/pod-product-compliance
Lightning Source LLC
Chambersburg PA
CBHW071951260326
41914CB00004B/797